AUNG SAN SUU KYI

AND BURMA'S STRUGGLE FOR DEMOCRACY

AUNG SAN SUU KYI
AND BURMA'S STRUGGLE FOR DEMOCRACY

BERTIL LINTNER

SILKWORM BOOKS

ISBN: 978-616-215-015-9

This English edition published in 2011 by
Silkworm Books
6 Sukkasem Road, T. Suthep
Chiang Mai 50200 Thailand
info@silkwormbooks.com
http://www.silkwormbooks.com

Typeset by Silk Type in Minion Pro 10.5 pt.

Printed and bound in China

10 9 8 7 6 5 4 3 2

CONTENTS

ABBREVIATIONS

ABSDF	All-Burma Students Democratic Front. Anti-government student organization set up in the border areas after the 1988 uprising.
AFPFL	Anti-Fascist People's Freedom League. Burma's main political party in the 1940s and 1950s.
BSPP	Burma Socialist Programme Party. The only legally permitted political party from 1962 to 1988.
CPB	Communist Party of Burma. Founded in 1939, in rebellion against the government from 1948 to 1989.
CRDB	Committee for the Restoration of Democracy in Burma. Thai-border-based group of Burmese exiles in the late 1980s, now defunct.
DAB	Democratic Alliance of Burma. Alliance between the ethnic rebels and pro-democracy Burmese, set up on the Thai border in 1988. Now defunct.
KIA	Kachin Independence Army. Kachin rebel group, now has a ceasefire agreement with the government.
KKY	Ka Kwe Ye (literally, "defense"). Government-backed home guard units in the 1960s and 1970s which were allowed to trade in opium.
KNU	Karen National Union. Karen rebel group. Went underground in 1949 and is still in rebellion against the government.
NCGUB	National Coalition Government of the Union of Burma. Set up on the Thai border in late 1990 by NLD MPs-elect and some ethnic rebel groups.
NDF	National Democratic Force. Formed by members of the NLD who broke away and decided to participate in the November 2010 election.
NDF	National Democratic Front. Alliance of several ethnic rebel groups set up on the Thai border in 1976. Now defunct.

NLD	National League for Democracy. Pro-democracy party formed in 1988. Won a landslide victory in 1990, but was not allowed to form a government.
NUP	National Unity Party. The new name of the BSPP since 1988.
RGH	Rangoon General Hospital. Rangoon's main hospital where the dead and wounded were brought after the August 1988 massacre.
SLORC	State Law and Order Restoration Council. Burma's ruling junta, 1988-1997.
SPDC	State Peace and Development Council. The new name of the junta since 1997.
SSA	Shan State Army. Shan rebel group, still fighting the government.
USDA	Union Solidarity and Development Association. Pro-military support group set up in 1993. Became the Union Solidarity and Development Party (USDP) in June 2010 to enable it to take part in elections five months later.
UWSA	United Wa State Army. Amalgamation of the Wa forces of the former CPB and Thai-border-based Wa rebels.

Aung San and Daw Khin Kyi at their wedding, September 6, 1942.

General Aung San and his three children: Aung San Suu Kyi, Aung San U, and Aung San Lin.

Aung San and Gen. Ne Win during World War II.

Aung San Suu Kyi studying at St. Hugh's College, Oxford.

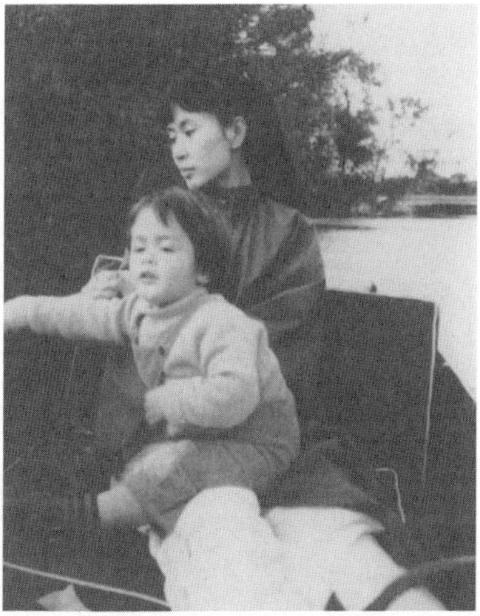

Aung San Suu Kyi and her son Kim in Oxford.

Aung San Suu Kyi and Michael Aris at their wedding in 1972.

On August 8, 1988 (8.8.88), hundreds of thousands of people took to the streets in Rangoon.

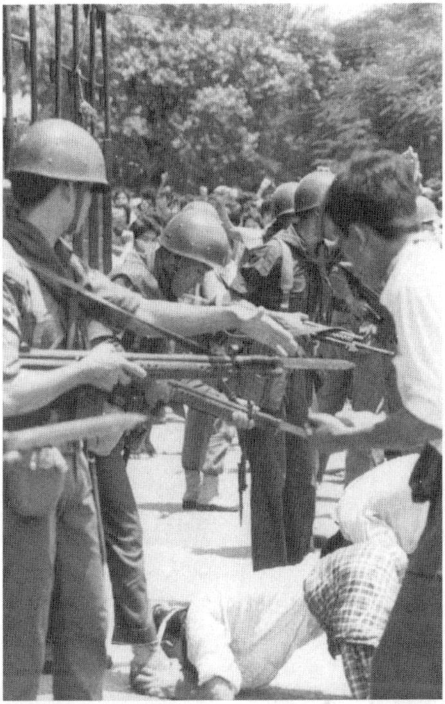

Demonstrators begged the troops not to shoot on 8.8.88. Later that day, the soldiers opened fire anyway. (Photo by Ryo Takeda)

A barricade in Rangoon after the massacre, August 8–9, 1988. Thousands of people were shot by the army. (Photo by Peter Conard)

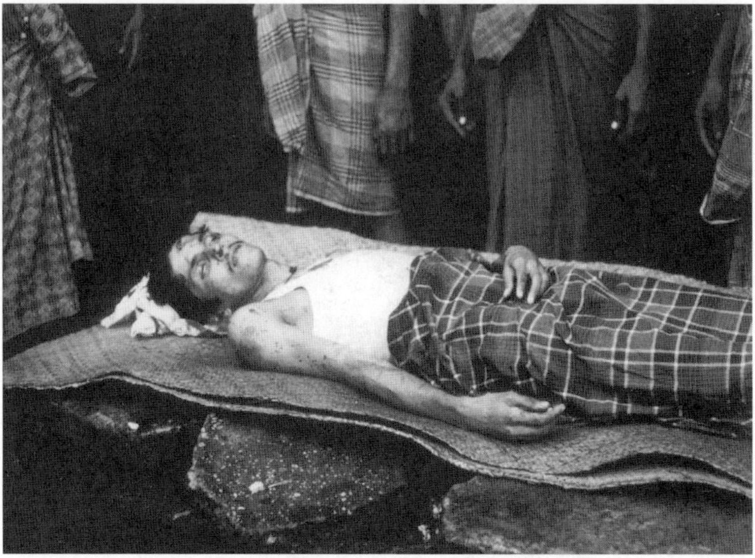

One of many victims of the August 8–10, 1988, massacre. This young man was shot in downtown Rangoon during the night between August 8 and 9. (Photo by Peter Conard)

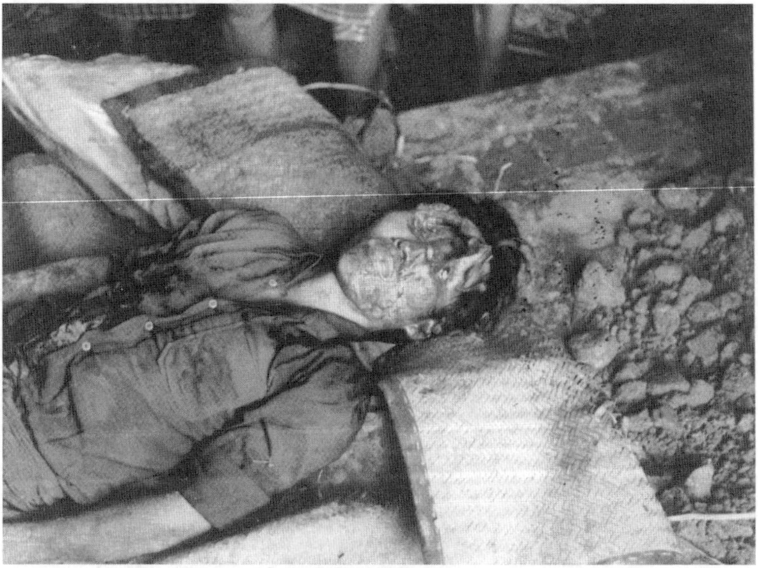

Another victim of the August 8–10 massacre. This man was shot in the head by a high-powered gun. The government claimed they were "looters." (Photo by Peter Conard)

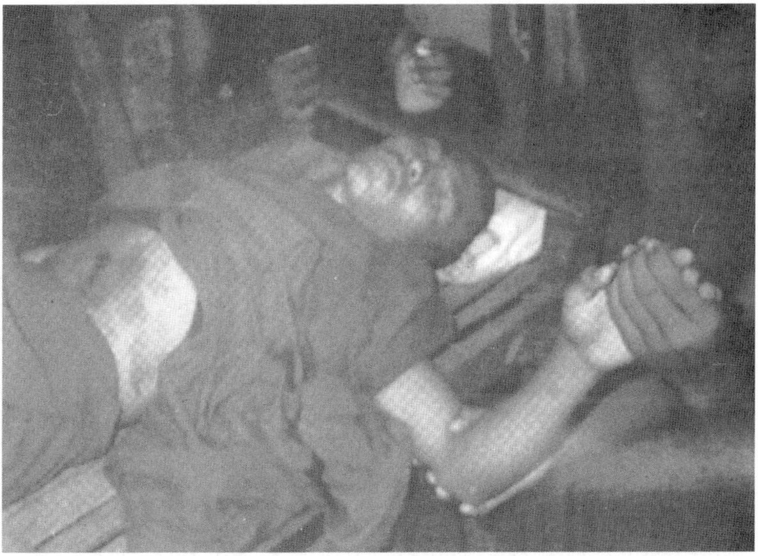

In Sagaing, near Mandalay, even monks were killed
when the military opened fire on the protesters, August 9, 1988.

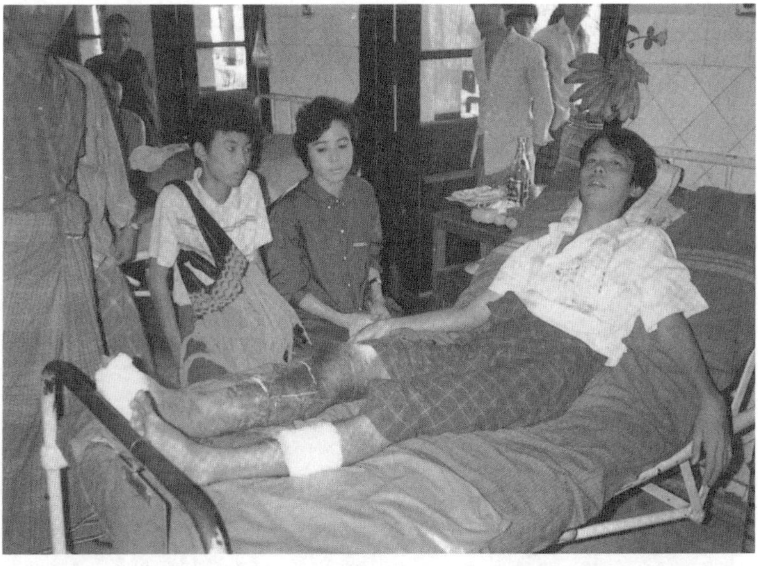

A young man brought to Rangoon General Hospital with a leg injury after the August 8–10 massacre. He was a lucky survivor; most gunshot victims were shot and killed.
(Photo by Peter Conard)

Buddhist monks join the demonstrations, August 1988.

Young people demonstrating in Rangoon, August 1988.

Student leader Min Ko Naing at the founding of the All-Burma Federation of Student Unions (ABFSU), August 28, 1988.

Women demonstrating in Rangoon, August 1988.

Poster in Rangoon during the August–September 1988 uprising. Army chief Gen. Saw Maung is depicted as a loyal and obedient dog.

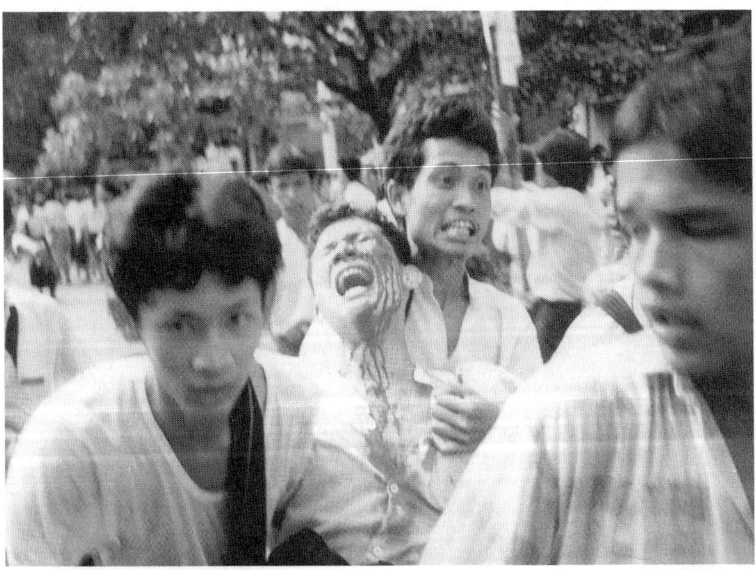

Someone—it is not clear who—opened fire on demonstrators in Rangoon during a protest in early September 1988, before the military moved in to reassert power on September 18.

Even schoolchildren demonstrated in August and September 1988.

The killings did not stop the demonstrations. People from all walks of life joined the protests in August–September 1988.

Air force men at Mingaladon air force base north of Rangoon joined the uprising, September 1988.

Servicemen who joined the demonstrations were welcomed by Buddhist monks, Rangoon, September 1988.

Anti-government protesters gather outside Sule Pagoda in downtown Rangoon, early September 1988.

People's Railway Police joined the pro-democracy demonstrations, Rangoon, September 1988.

In 1989 Aung San Suu Kyi was able to travel around the country relatively freely. Here, she is at a rally in a small town in central Burma.

Huge crowds welcomed her.

Aung San Suu Kyi is followed by an armed soldier, 1989.

Aung San Suu Kyi addresses a rally in Myitkyina, Kachin State, 1989.

Aung San Suu Kyi addresses a meeting in Rangoon, April 1989. (Photo by author)

Zagarnar, Burma's most famous comedian (standing), played an important role in the 1988 uprising and afterwards. He was arrested in 2008 and is now imprisoned in the far north of the country.

Shan State Army, one of many ethnic rebel armies in the country
(Photo by author)

After the military moved in to reassume power, thousands of pro-democracy activists fled to areas on the border controlled by ethnic insurgents. Phalu is an area south of the Thai border town of Mae Sot. (Photo by author)

INTRODUCTION

During the night of August 25, 1988—at the height of the pro-democracy uprising that shook Burma that year—a large crowd gathered at the foot of the Shwe Dagon Pagoda in the then capital Rangoon. Some had brought their bedrolls, and entire families squatted in circles around their evening meals. By mid-morning next day, several hundred thousand people of all ages, ethnic groups, and social classes in Burmese society had come together for what would be the biggest rally in the country's student-led movement for democracy. They were all there well in time to get a good vantage point for the meeting that had been announced for the twenty-sixth: Aung San Suu Kyi, the forty-three-year-old daughter of Burma's independence hero Aung San, was going to address the crowd.

The slim, professorial woman had returned to Burma from her home in Oxford, England, in April to nurse her sick mother and was followed a few months later by her English husband, Michael Aris, and their two sons. They arrived at a time when the country was in the midst of political upheaval. Student protests had led to the most serious threat to the iron-fisted rule of the strongman at the time, General Ne Win, since he had overthrown Burma's democratically elected government and seized power in March 1962.

The mood was festive but there were several bomb scares before the actual meeting began. Students and Buddhist monks were taking care of the security and formed human chains around the stage where she was going to appear. They spent more than three hours searching the stage and checking on suspicious-looking characters. The ground outside the pagoda complex was jam-packed. All roads leading up to the meeting place were full of people.

A huge portrait of Suu Kyi's father, Aung San, had been placed above the stage alongside a resistance flag from World War II. Loudspeakers were directed towards the enormous crowd. Eventually she arrived. Her car had to stop outside the meeting ground since there were so many people, and she walked the remaining stretch up to the stage amidst deafening applause and cheers. Htun Wai, a well-known Burmese film actor, introduced Aung San Suu Kyi and told the restive crowd to sit down and listen to her speech.

It was the first major political address for Aung San Suu Kyi, who was present at this crucial time in Burma's modern history by accident. Yet she was confident, slipping easily into the heritage of her politician father. She moved from an initial message of democracy through unity to a more personal note:

> A number of people are saying that since I've spent most of my life abroad and am married to a foreigner, I could not be familiar with the ramifications of this country's politics. I wish to speak to you very frankly and openly. It's true that I've lived abroad. It's also true that I'm married to a foreigner. But these facts have never, and will never, interfere with or lessen my love and devotion for my country by any measure or degree. People have been saying that I know nothing of Burmese politics. The trouble is I know too much. My family knows better than any how devious Burmese politics can be and how much my father had to suffer on this account.[1]

Hundreds of thousands of people cheered and applauded. Her famous, almost deified father had been assassinated by a rival politician on July 19, 1947, barely six months before Burma's independence from Britain, when Aung San Suu Kyi was only two years old. The roar reached its crescendo when she concluded, "The present crisis is the concern of the entire nation. I could not, as my father's daughter, remain indifferent to all that was going on. This national crisis could, in fact, be called the second struggle for independence."

Most of the people who had come to see her outside the Shwe Dagon had probably done so out of curiosity. But during her speech the daughter of Burma's foremost hero won the hearts of her audience. She emerged as the leading voice for the opposition that demanded the restoration of democracy in the country. "We were all surprised," a participant in the meeting commented much later. Not only did she look like her father, she spoke like him as well: short, concise, and right to the point."[2]

Aung San Suu Kyi's intervention had actually begun eleven days before her first public appearance with a personal letter to the secretary of the State Council, General Kyaw Htin, who had become acting head of state following the resignation on August 12 of Ne Win's trusted protégé, Sein Lwin. He, in turn, had served as Burma's president for only eighteen days—from the time of Ne Win's resignation from his post as chairman of the country's only legally permitted political organization, the Burma Socialist Programme Party (BSPP), on July 23. Sein Lwin's short reign had been marked by almost daily street protests—and the massacre of thousands of unarmed demonstrators.

The letter was supported by a number of former state leaders of the pre-1962 era, including the erstwhile prime minister U Nu and ex-president Mahn Win Maung. It stated that "a situation of ugliness unmatched since Burma regained her independence arose throughout the country," and it suggested the formation of a "People's Consultative Committee" to deal with the crisis. This committee did not demand the resignation of the government but called for a dialogue between the authorities and various veteran politicians and well-known public figures. The government, however, did not respond but carried on as if nothing had happened.

Until this letter was sent—and the decisive mass meeting outside the Shwe Dagon that followed—Burma's pro-democracy uprising had been completely spontaneous, and it had lacked proper leadership. Now, a leader was emerging who commanded increasing admiration and support. Her insistence on Gandhian principles of nonviolent confrontation came to play a crucial role in transforming the Burmese uprising into a sustained and remarkably coordinated movement.

This became even more apparent after September 18, 1988, when the military led by the chief of staff, General Saw Maung, decided to step in—not to overthrow a failing government, but to shore up a regime overwhelmed by popular protests. Thousands of people were massacred once again as heavily armed troops opened fire on demonstrators in Rangoon and elsewhere across the country.

But somewhat surprisingly, after suppressing the pro-democracy movement of 1988, General Saw Maung's new junta, the so-called "State Law and Order Restoration Council," with its ominous-sounding acronym, SLORC, also announced that it intended to honor the pledge of the previous government—which had been led by Sein Lwin's successor, Dr. Maung Maung—to hold "free and fair elections."

On September 22, the country's powerful military intelligence chief, Brig.-Gen. Khin Nyunt, made a solemn pledge before a gathering of foreign military attachés in Rangoon: "Elections will be held as soon as law and order has been restored and the Defence Services will then systematically hand over power to the party which wins."[3] He didn't say a word about the need to draft a new constitution, which later became the military government's excuse for not handing over power to the party that won. It may seem incongruous that a military government that had seized power by force would insist on a constitution and other legalities, but that was exactly what the Burmese military did. Meanwhile, it continued to exercise absolute power—without a constitution.

Burma's previous socialist system was formally abolished, and a multi-party system replaced the former one-party rule of the BSPP. But a notorious martial law decree issued by the SLORC and named 2/88 banned public gatherings of five or more people. The military also firmly controlled the media; there was only one newspaper, the SLORC's own propaganda sheet, the *Working People's Daily*. Within the strict limitations of the new martial law regime, however, the Burmese pro-democracy movement continued the struggle that had begun months before.

On September 24, the National League for Democracy (NLD), was formed officially. Aung Gyi, a retired brigadier-general of the Burma

Army who to some extent had initiated the movement by writing and widely distributing a series of open letters to Ne Win, was chairman. Tin U, an ex-general and erstwhile army chief of staff who had been ousted and jailed by Ne Win in 1976, was elected vice chairman. But it was the NLD's general secretary, Aung San Suu Kyi, who became the most popular spokesperson for the league. Her role as Burma's foremost opposition leader was further enhanced when Aung Gyi decided to split with the NLD in December 1988 to set up his own organization, the oddly named Union Nationals Democracy Party (UNDP).

However, Aung Gyi's new party failed to win any significant popular support; Aung San Suu Kyi was now almost alone in challenging the military regime. Her NLD became increasingly consolidated on explicitly nonviolent principles, and the party grew to become Burma's largest political organization with a membership of at least two million. She traveled around the country and attracted crowds of tens of thousands wherever she went, even in remote country towns. The challenge became so serious that the SLORC decided to place her under house arrest on July 20, 1989, less than a year after her first speech outside the Shwe Dagon Pagoda.

The SLORC had hoped that the crackdown in July 1989 would cripple the NLD. Not only Aung San Suu Kyi, but also vice chairman Tin U and a number of other prominent leaders, were interned. Some were sentenced to long prison terms and thrown into Rangoon's notorious Insein Prison.

With Aung San Suu Kyi incarcerated in her own house in Rangoon, the SLORC evidently felt more secure, and were confident that the threat posed by her outspoken criticism of military excesses had been eliminated. So they decided to go ahead with the general election they had promised when the SLORC was set up on September 18 the year before. Probably believing that its year-long propaganda campaign in the *Working People's Daily* against her and the NLD had been effective—and evidently underestimating the degree of hatred towards the military that still existed—the SLORC also decided to allow an astonishing degree of openness following months of repression and harassment of political activists. Even foreign journalists were invited to cover the election and there were no reports of tampering with the voting registers or ballot boxes.

The SLORC had seriously misjudged the situation. When the Burmese people on May 27, 1990, at last were given the chance to freely elect their own representatives for the first time since 1960, two years before the initial military takeover, they voted overwhelmingly for the NLD. It captured 392 of the 485 seats contested in the 492-member National Assembly that was being elected. (Elections were postponed in seven constituencies for security reasons.) The rest went to NLD allies from the various minority areas, while the military-backed National Unity Party (NUD)—the new name for the BSPP—captured a mere ten seats. Only one candidate from Aung Gyi's UNDP was elected.

The NLD's landslide victory was a clear indication that Aung San Suu Kyi's year-long campaign, from August 1988 to July 1989, had produced remarkable results not only in terms of support for her party. There was not a single incident of violence or misbehavior on the part of the public on election day. The Burmese went to the polls with unity and dignity.

"Burmese throughout the country were often unaware of the NLD candidate they were actually voting for. But they had all heard of Aung San Suu Kyi. It was yes to her and no to Ne Win," *Time* magazine wrote in a cover story immediately after the astonishing elections in Burma.[4] Although the Burmese military was officially led by the SLORC chairman, Saw Maung, few Burmese doubted that it was the supposedly retired Ne Win who was still pulling the strings—in the same way that Aung San Suu Kyi, despite her detention, personified the NLD and Burma's mass movement for democracy.

The SLORC was probably as taken aback as almost everybody else; it was utterly unprepared for an NLD victory of this magnitude. The NLD won even in Rangoon's Dagon township, which includes the capital's cantonment area and the SLORC headquarters, and on the Coco Islands, a naval base in the Bay of Bengal that is off-limits for ordinary civilians. Only naval personnel and support services are based there. The leader of the NUP, Tha Kyaw, a former BSPP minister, was also defeated by the NLD in his constituency in Hmawbi, near a major army camp and an air force base. For this reason, political observers noted after the election that whatever the military leadership decided to do, it would have to tread carefully so as not to provoke a backlash from its own rank and file, who apparently also had voted for the NLD.

Many Burmese at the time pointed out that the election—in which actually more than ninety political parties participated—should not be viewed as a Western-style poll with different parties competing for seats. Rather, it was a referendum in which the NLD represented the democratic aspirations of the vast majority of the Burmese people and the NUP stood for the old system.

The SLORC, however, once again demonstrated its intransigence and that it was determined to cling to power through threats and brutal force. Intelligence chief Khin Nyunt appeared again on July 27, singing a different tune from that of September 1988. He now claimed that a "constituent assembly," vested only with the task of drafting a new constitution, had been elected, not a parliament. He added:

> It should not be necessary to explain that a political organization does not automatically obtain the three sovereign powers of the legislative, administrative and judicial powers by the emergence of a Pyithu Hluttaw [parliament]. . . . Only the SLORC has the right to legislative power. . . . Drafting an interim constitution to obtain state power and to form a government will not be accepted in any way and if it is done effective action will be taken according to the law.[5]

In spite of the NLD's landslide victory at the polls, it was becoming clear that the SLORC had no intention to hand over power to anyone.

Drafting a constitution was not a major issue before the election, even if Saw Maung on a couple of occasions had mentioned the need for a new charter. But he had also said in a speech to the nation on January 9, 1990, four and a half months before the election:

> We have spoken on the matter of State power. As soon as the election is held, form a government according to law and then take power. An election has to be held to bring forth a government. That is our responsibility. But the actual work of forming a legal government after the election is not

> the duty of the Tatmadaw [the armed forces]. We are saying it very clearly and candidly right now.[6]

He had also lashed out against the pro-democracy movement for raising the issue of a constitution before the people went to the polls. In a speech on May 10—two weeks prior to the election—he stated, "A dignitary who once was an Attorney-General talked about the importance of the constitution. As our current aim is to hold the election as scheduled we cannot as yet concern ourselves with the constitution as mentioned by that person. Furthermore, it is not our concern. A new constitution can be drafted. An old constitution can also be used after some amendments."[7]

The "dignitary" referred to was former Attorney-General U Hla Aung, who was close to the NLD and, at the time, was researching constitutional issues for the pro-democracy movement.[8]

All this was conveniently forgotten when the NLD had won the election. Dismayed at the complete turnaround and the broken promises, on the day after Khin Nyunt's speech, the NLD members who had been elected to the assembly met at the Gandhi Hall in Rangoon's Kyauktada township. They adopted a resolution calling on the SLORC to stand down and hand over power to a democratically elected government. During the interim period, "the people shall, as a minimum, enjoy the freedom of publication and expression. It is against political nature that the NLD, which has overwhelmingly won enough seats in the Pyithu Hluttaw to form a government, itself has been prohibited the minimum of democratic rights," the Gandhi Hall Declaration stated. It also called for "frank and sincere discussions with good faith and with the object of national reconciliation."[9]

But the SLORC did not budge or even consider a dialogue, and when it became clear that the generals were not going to respect the outcome of the election, and that the NLD and the general public were in no position to alter the military's stance, Burma's *sangha*, the order of monks, took the initiative. On August 8, 1990, the second anniversary of the 1988 uprising, thousands of Buddhist monks marched through the streets of the northern city of Mandalay.

It was not officially a demonstration—the monks were out on their morning alms round—but the choice of the date and the vast number of monks who took part in the procession made the intention obvious enough. Tens of thousands of people showed up in the streets to offer food to the monks while nervous soldiers looked on. At one point along the route, some students hoisted a peacock flag, the symbol of the Burmese nationalists during the British colonial era and now also of the pro-democracy movement.

Some soldiers apparently overreacted. They opened fire with their automatic G-3 rifles, and bullets ripped through the crowd. Shi Ah Sein Na, a seventeen-year-old novice from Mogaung monastery in Mandalay, was wounded as bullets punctured one of his lungs and shattered his shoulder. He fell to the ground, bleeding profusely.

Nine more monks and at least two onlookers were also hit. Alms bowls broken by bullets lay in the street while the soldiers charged the crowd. Fourteen monks were badly beaten, and at least five were arrested. Several of the wounded went missing. Some were presumed dead.[10]

The brutality against the monks appalled everyone. To add insult to injury, the authorities in Rangoon flatly denied that any shooting had occurred in Mandalay. The state-run radio claimed that the students and the monks had attacked the security forces and that one novice had been slightly injured in the commotion.[11]

The official whitewash of the incident was not accepted by the monks in Mandalay. On August 27, more than seven thousand monks gathered in the city. They decided to refuse to accept offerings from soldiers and their families, or to perform religious rites for them, in effect excommunicating anyone associated with the military. The boycott soon spread all over Mandalay and to other towns in upper Burma: Sagaing, Monywa, Pakokku, Myingyan, Meiktila, Shwebo, and Ye-U.

In Rangoon, two thousand monks met at the Buddhist study center of Ngar Htat Gyi to join the campaign against the military. The conflict with the monks was the most serious challenge to the military thus far: the boycott affected the ordinary soldiers and their families, and the loyalty of the rank and file was crucial for the survival of the SLORC. It was also not forgotten that most of the troops had actually voted for the NLD in the election in May.

Again the SLORC decided to use force to quell the dissent. In the early hours of September 7, Kyi Maung, a retired army officer who had acted as head of the NLD since the incarceration of Aung San Suu Kyi and Tin U, was detained on trumped up charges along with what remained of the party's top leadership. In the weeks that followed, more than sixty-five MPs-elect were arrested, while more than twenty fled to the borders with Thailand and India.[12]

Few people believed that the army would dare move against the Buddhist monks. But it did. On October 20, SLORC chairman Saw Maung ordered the dissolution of all Buddhist organizations involved in anti-government activities. "Those who refuse will not be allowed to remain monks," he stated.[13] Local military commanders were vested with martial law powers, enabling them to disrobe monks and have them imprisoned or executed if they did not comply with the SLORC decree.

Two days later, leaflets ordering the monks to give up the boycott were dropped from army helicopters over several Mandalay monasteries. Then the army moved into action. One hundred and thirty-three monasteries were raided by heavily armed troops, and scores of monks were led away into captivity.[14] Saw Maung, who had traveled to Mandalay to conduct the action against the monks, returned to Rangoon on October 24 after ending the operation successfully. Among those arrested were some of Burma's most respected senior abbots, including U Thumingala, head of a renowned teaching monastery in Rangoon.

In many ways, the last hope for the democratic opposition had been pinned on the monks. When the army demonstrated that it did not hesitate to move against the most respected segment of Burmese society, many people lost heart. The pro-democracy movement crumbled, and all overt opposition to the SLORC ceased, never to be the same again.

Burma's political conflict was far from over, however. Towards the end of 1991 Burma was headline news again. Aung San Suu Kyi was awarded the most prestigious of international honors, the Nobel Peace Prize. Though under house arrest, Burma's most prominent dissident joined the likes of Tibet's Dalai Lama, Calcutta's Mother Teresa, South

African bishop Desmond Tutu, and American civil rights pioneer Martin Luther King.

Then, it seems, everything went wrong. Fifteen years later, the Burmese military was more firmly entrenched than at any time since it first seized power in 1962. The United Nations and its various subcommittees adopted resolutions calling upon Burma's military regime to enter into a dialogue with the pro-democracy movement. Spokespersons for many foreign countries did the same and more. But, hardly surprisingly, the junta in Rangoon just ignored the groundswell of criticism from abroad. The generals make their own decisions, regardless of what the outside world says or thinks.

On July 10, 1995, Suu Kyi was released from house arrest and she was able to tour the country again, campaigning for democracy. Gradually, however, the military began to curtail her movements, and she was placed under house arrest again in September 2000. Following mediation by a special UN envoy to Burma, Malaysian diplomat Razali Ismail, she was released on May 6, 2002. But that freedom did not last long. On May 30, 2003, a military-sponsored crowd of thugs attacked her entourage as it was traveling through Depayin district north of Mandalay. Scores of NLD supporters were killed, and hundreds were arrested and imprisoned. Suu Kyi was taken into "protective custody" and escorted back to Rangoon, yet again placed under house arrest. There she remained until November 2010, and the once massive popular movement for democracy, the NLD, is only a bleak shadow of what it was in the late 1980s and early 1990s.

Most young activists have been imprisoned, cowed into submission, or have fled the country. Only a handful of mostly elderly spokespersons remain, and none of them has the strength and charisma to carry the party forward. That serves the interests of the junta, which in November 1997 had been renamed "the State Peace and Development Council" (SPDC), since the new-look NLD would appear to the outside world not to be a viable alternative to the present order.

And Suu Kyi? The Joan of Arc of Burma, Asia's Nelson Mandela, the "female bodhisattva" who, to the Burmese public at large, symbolized a heroine like the mythical mother goddess of the earth who could "free them from the enslavement of the evil military captors?"[15] A cult has grown up around her and she has had some hand in its growth.[16] Between November 1995 and December 1996, when she was relatively free to move about, speak in public, and write, she had a weekly column in the *Mainichi Daily* in Japan; the pieces appeared disjointed and, to many readers, puzzling, with their mix of Buddhist philosophy, Burmese folklore, and sometimes hazy descriptions of the political scene in her country.

Suu Kyi's almost mystical streak makes her writings, and most books about her, different from those by and about other democratic leaders who have spent time in prison, such as Mandela, the Czech democracy hero Vaclav Havel, and India's Mahatma Gandhi, who was not just a saint but also a shrewd politician. Suu Kyi may indeed be a good saint, but when asked a question about her politics by American interviewer Alan Clements, she replied, "I never discuss our future plans."[17] Unfortunately, Suu Kyi's lack of a comprehensive political plan of action for Burma may fail to prevent more tragedies from happening and may stall the re-emergence of a credible force that can challenge the present regime and appeal to the international community.

It is also an open question to what extent Suu Kyi fully appreciates the complexities of Burma's ethnic conflicts. The country has dozens of ethnic minorities speaking a multitude of languages and dialects. In a speech delivered to a meeting held in Myitkyina, Kachin State, on April 27, 1989, she said, "At this time there is very great need for all our ethnic groups to be joined together. We cannot have the attitude of 'I'm Kachin,' 'I'm Burman,' 'I'm Shan.' We must have the attitude that we are all comrades in the struggle for democratic rights."[18]

Judging from the faces of the local participants at the meeting, there were few takers.[19] Ethnic pride and identity are more important to most people in the frontier areas than what kind of political system prevails in the, for them, distant capital in the central Burmese plains.

At the same time, appeals for a dialogue and national reconciliation from the UN and the international community—and attempts at "constructive engagement" by its partners in the Association of Southeast Asian Nations "ASEAN"—are not likely to produce any tangible results. The junta makes its own decisions and listens to nobody.

The main reason for the regime's uncompromising stand is simple: over their many years in power—since 1962— the generals and other military men have committed what the rest of the world, and domestic opinion, would consider serious crimes against humanity, including murder, theft of people's property and public funds, rape, and collusion with drug traffickers. They have too much to hide, and nothing is to be gained from allowing more openness and transparency. Or, as one Rangoon-based Western diplomat once put it to me quite bluntly, "They fear that if they don't hang together, they'll hang separately."

The fear of retribution is so strong that when after the 1990 election Kyi Maung, then the NLD's acting head, said in an interview with the Hong Kong magazine *Asiaweek* that "here in Burma we do not need any Nuremberg-style tribunal," or words to that effect, he was promptly arrested.[20] The very mentioning of Nuremberg scared the generals.

While some degree of political pluralism among the population at large was permitted during the darkest years of military dictatorship in, for instance, Thailand and Indonesia, the Burmese military has always exercised absolute power and enjoyed a position that is far more privileged than its Asian counterparts. In fact, during decades in power, the Burmese military has created a parallel state within the state, a society where army personnel, and their families and dependents, are isolated from the rest of the population.

In Burma, there are special schools and hospitals for army personnel and their families, they live in secluded, subsidized housing, and they can buy goods that are not available in ordinary stores. An army pass assures the holder of a seat in a train or on an airplane, and a policeman would never dare to report a member of the military for violating traffic rules.

In November 2005, the junta even moved the capital to a secluded location near Pyinmana, nearly 400 kilometers north of Rangoon. An entirely new city is being built in what until then was jungle—and ordinary citizens do not have the right to enter without special permission. Called Naypyidaw, meaning "capital" or "place of a king" in old-fashioned usage, it is populated entirely by soldiers and government officials. Typically, only foreign defense attachés, not civilian diplomats, were invited to attend the Armed Forces Day celebrations, when they were held there for the first time on March 27, 2006.

Democracy would deprive the ruling elite—which in Burma is synonymous with the military—of its privileges. Democracy is a threat to the existing order. There are now more than four hundred thousand men in Burma's armed forces, and if close family members are included, the total would be approximately two million people. They are prepared to suppress any movement for democracy, as they did in 1988, 1990, and 2003.

Sooner or later, change may come to Burma, but it would have to come from a change of mind from some elements within the armed forces. Given the resistance that could be expected to any challenge to the status quo from mainstream military, the outcome could be violent, and perhaps even result in civil war.

Collapse of the regime could also lead to anarchy and chaos, as there are no power centers in the country other than the military. The country has not had a civilian government since 1962 and lacks people with administrative skills and experience. The NLD today is too weak to govern the country. Given the country's ethnic diversity, it could fall apart as Yugoslavia did after the death of Marshal Tito.

Is Suu Kyi prepared for this? Could she hold the country together if chaos broke out? The Burmese people want freedom, but is she able to lead them to that goal? A critical look at Suu Kyi, her strengths and weaknesses, is essential if we want to know what the future holds for Burma. This book is such an attempt at a better understanding of who she is, where she comes from, and what she stands for.

Some Burmese readers may find this account of her role in the country's pro-democracy movement somewhat offensive because it includes negative remarks about her and the NLD. But constructive criticism is the lifeblood of any functioning democracy; without it, democracy would become stale and lose its vibrancy. And I am certain Suu Kyi herself would feel uncomfortable with what I call her "deification." She has always been too humble and down-to-earth for that. No one is doing her any favor by elevating her to some lofty position to which she does not belong. She is, after all, a human being like the rest of us. And she is Burma's only hope for a better future. The ecstatic reaction of the public to her release from house arrest in November 2010 shows that she has not, as some of her detractors like to claim, had her day, and been relegated to the past.

CHAPTER 1

THE LEGACY

Aung San Suu Kyi was born in Rangoon on June 19, 1945, a Tuesday. The day of the week on which a child is born is important in Burmese popular belief. The child's name must begin with one of certain letters belonging to that particular day, and it is commonly believed that the day of birth will influence the child's character. A Tuesday-born child will be honest while one born on a Saturday is doomed to be hot-tempered and quarrelsome. Suu Kyi's father, Aung San, was born on a Saturday and so was U Nu, independent Burma's first prime minister.[1]

This belief may seem like superstition to most non-Burmese, but it is so strong that it molds an individual's personality as he or she grows up. Suu Kyi knew already as a child that she was expected to be honest and ethical. People expected her father to stir up trouble, and so he did. Born in 1915 in Natmauk, a township just north of the Pegu Yoma mountains in central Burma, he was considered a bright child, and in 1932 he entered Rangoon University, where he also became involved in radical political movements. In his own words, "Twice, at the University, I was threatened with expulsion for fighting for the rights of fellow students. In fact, it was my suspension for three years which touched off the students' strike of 1936."[2]

The student movement, whose stated aim was independence for Burma from its British colonial masters, was to a large extent inspired by a rebellion in 1930–31 led by a former Buddhist monk called U Yar

Kyaw. He had organized secret societies in the Burmese countryside, and his followers, known as *galon* after a powerful bird in Hindu mythology, believed that their tattoos and amulets would make them invulnerable to British bullets. Most of them were village youths and others were from the impoverished countryside, which the splendors of the colonial economy never reached. They were poor and they were desperate.[3]

U Yar Kyaw proclaimed himself king under the name Saya San and, assuming the presumptuous title of "Thupannaka Galuna Raja" (Illustrious Galon King), he raised an army of disgruntled peasants. Equipped with handmade shotguns manufactured from pipe lengths and bicycle tubing, crossbows, and spears, they faced the modern guns of the British army.

The colonial government's forces resorted to brutal suppression: entire villages were razed to the ground, suspected rebels were decapitated, and their severed heads displayed as a warning to others. In just one particularly gruesome incident, fifteen severed heads were displayed in front of the deputy commissioner's office in the town of Prome. Photographs of the gory exhibition appeared in the *Thuriya* (Sun) newspaper, owned and edited by U Saw, a prominent Burmese politician and an ardent admirer of Saya San, and copies were sent to the British parliament.[4]

When the uprising was finally crushed, more than 10,000 rebels had been killed, 9,000 captured alive and imprisoned, and 128 hanged—including Saya San himself and two of his closest associates, Saya Nyan, and a hermit called Bandaka. Saya San went to the gallows with his head held high on November 28, 1931. On the government's side there had been no more than fifty casualties. In her book *Freedom from Fear*, Aung San Suu Kyi noted that the Saya San rebellion aroused "the patriotic sympathy of the people who were also repelled by the ruthlessness with which the British dealt with the rebels."[5]

To uphold the glory of Saya San's *galon*, U Saw in 1938 raised his own force, named after the rebel leader's ragtag band of peasant rebels. The cadres of his new "Galon Tat" (Galon Force) wore green uniforms and carried bamboo staves. It also inspired the young minds of the students in Rangoon, Aung San among them. Saya San was a traditional *minlaung* (pretender to the throne)—a figure who often arose in times of crisis in Burma—and he wanted a return to the old Buddhist kingdom of precolonial days. But the young nationalists did not miss the point that most of Saya San's followers were monks and impoverished farmers, and the rebellion had clearly demonstrated their potential. Until then, the Burmese nationalist movement had been confined to intellectual circles in Rangoon, Mandalay, and other major cities.

The injustice of colonial rule and the awareness of the suffering of the agrarian population that had manifested itself in the Saya San rebellion made the young nationalists open to leftist thinking; the view that socialism was opposed to colonialism and imperialism made these ideas even more attractive in the 1930s.[6] Paradoxically, the royalties from a book written by the royalist magician Saya San provided the funds to establish a library with the first Marxist literature to reach Burma. The young nationalists were avid readers, and the authors whose work they studied included Marx, Lenin, Nehru, Sun Yat Sen, Garibaldi, Voltaire, Rousseau, Upton Sinclair, John Strachey, John Reed, and various writers from Ireland's Sinn Fein movement. The nationalists were young but sufficiently educated to realize that there was no returning to the Burmese monarchy, so they were drawn to the utopia of a socialist state.

Most of this literature was brought in by students returning from England, and a number of book clubs, notably the Nagani (Red Dragon) Book Club, were set up in Rangoon and elsewhere. A glance at the list of books published by the Nagani Book Club shows that among the 101 titles, there were 38 on war, 36 on nationalism, and 31 on the Irish nationalist leader Michael Collins. There was one book on Nehru, two on Gandhi, two on De Valera, three on Stalin, four on Hitler and six on Lenin.[7]

"The revolutionary, leftist bias of the club was in little doubt," Suu Kyi wrote much later.[8] On August 15, 1939—following strikes among students at Rangoon University and workers in the Yenangyaung oil fields southwest of Mandalay—a group of radical students met in a small flat in Barr Street, Rangoon, and founded the Communist Party of Burma (CPB). Among them was Aung San, who was elected general secretary.[9] At the time, leftist ideas were widespread in Burma, and in many ways dominated the student movement. At the same time, however, Buddhist beliefs and Burmese authoritarian traditions flourished, sometimes side by side with socialism and communism.

The confusion of the 1930s reflected an extremely complicated historical dichotomy, which has always been Burma's dilemma. Saya San stood for Burma's age-old authoritarian tradition. Although there is no doubt that the impetus his rebellion provided helped pave the way for Burma's independence movement, it nevertheless represented the past, "an armed enterprise relying on the call of racial pride and the charisma of the leader," to quote Aung San Suu Kyi's own study of the topic.[10]

According to American Burma scholar, Josef Silverstein, a Burmese king was

> shielded from the eyes of his subjects, wrapped in ritual, and responsible for the [Buddhist] faith; his authority was viewed as semi-divine and unbridled. . . . The state was therefore not a vehicle for social and economic change. If the state was venal—took an excessive amount of taxes or forced men to fight in needless wars—the individual could do little but to accept the situation. The political culture of the Burman early on was characterized by the people's stoic acceptance of misfortune and the government's excessive demands and victimization through theft, war, and plunder.[11]

By the ancient traditions of divine kingship, the monarch wielded unquestioned power over the life and death of his subjects. The values and beliefs of the people provided no basis for a doctrine of popular sovereignty.

The other side of Burma's heritage is represented by a solid intellectual and creative tradition. The yearly cycle in any Burmese village includes a number of *pwe*, usually translated as fairs, but which are actually much more than that. Every *pwe* worth mentioning includes a theatrical performance, and there are few people in the world who are so fond of culture and drama as the Burmese. Sir J. G. Scott, a Scotsman who wrote about Burma under the pseudonym Shway Yoe, aptly said that "probably there is no man, otherwise than a cripple, in the country, who has not at some period of his life been himself an actor, either in the drama or in a marionette show; if not in either of these, certainly in a chorus dance."[12]

Burma even prior to colonial times had a high literacy rate; education was a source of national pride long before the British came to the country in the nineteenth century. At the age of seven or eight, every Burmese boy was sent to the local Buddhist monastery to learn to read, write, and memorize chants and Pali formulas used in pagoda worship. For girls, education was less universal but even so, the census for British Burma in 1872 stated that "female education was a fact in Burma before Oxford was founded."[13]

Needless to say, the colonial authorities were mainly interested in procuring a stratum of English-speaking civil servants and skilled clerks to work in public administration and for foreign companies. But among the inevitable results was an abundance of newspapers and bookshops with foreign literature. A powerful intellectual and anti-authoritarian tendency began taking shape, which in many ways was as deeply rooted in Burmese tradition as the monarchic system.

The forward-looking nationalist movement, which reflected a fledgling Burmese renaissance of the intellectual tradition, was represented by the "Dohbama Asiayone" (We-Burmese Association). It had been set up in 1930, nine years before the CPB, and its leaders emerged as the most important statesmen in postwar Burma. They called themselves *thakin*, which actually means "master" and was a title set aside for the British, like "sahib" in India. By adding this to their names, the nationalists wanted to show who the real masters of their country were. The legacy of this dilemma lingers on, and even today authoritarian tendencies can be found in the pro-democracy student movement-in-exile as seen in sometimes violent purges, including executions, of dissidents within their own ranks.

When the Dohbama was established, there was debate among the young Burman nationalists as to what name should be used for the country: the formal, old royal term *Myanma*, or the more colloquial *Bama*, which the British had corrupted into "Burma" and made the official name of the colony.

The nationalists concluded:

> Since the Dohbama was set up, the movement always paid attention to the unity of all the nationalities of the country . . . and the *thakins* noted that *myanma naingngan* [the *myanma* state] . . . meant only the part of the country where the Burmans lived. This was the name given by the Burmese kings to their country. But this is not correct usage. *Bama naingngan* is not the country where only the *myanma* people live. It is the country where different nationalities such as the Kachin, Karen, Kayah, Chin, Pa-O, Palaung, Mon, Myanma, Rakhine, Shan reside. Therefore, the nationalists did not use the term *myanma naingngan* or *myanmapyi* [*myanma* country], but *bama naingngan* and *bamapyi*. All the nationalities who live in *bama naingngan* are called *bama*.[14]

Thus, the movement became the "Dohbama" instead of the "Dohmyanma." Half a century later, in 1989, Burma's new military rulers decided that the opposite was true and renamed the country "Myanmar": "*Bama* . . . is one of the national groups of the Union only. . . . *Myanma* means all the national racial groups who are resident of the union such as Kachin, Kayah, Karen, Chin, Mon, Rakhine, Bama, and Shan."[15]

A similar confusion exists in English where some scholars maintain that "Burman" refers to the majority people who inhabit the central plains whereas the term "Burmese" covers the language of the "Burmans"—as well as all citizens of the country, including the ethnic minorities. All these contradictions reflect an inescapable fact that many Burmans/Burmese are still reluctant to acknowledge: there is no term in any language that covers both the majority population and the ethnic minorities, as no such entity existed before the arrival of the British in the nineteenth century. Burma, or Myanmar, as we know it with all its present boundaries, is a colonial creation rife with internal contradictions and divisions.

Significantly, one of the few non-Burman members of the early nationalist movement was not a Shan or a Kachin, but M. A. Raschid, a Muslim of Indian origin. The other four in the leading "young quintet" were Thakin Aung San, Thakin Nu, Thakin Kyaw Nyein, and Thakin Thein Pe—all left-leaning student activists. At the time, almost half of Rangoon's population—and most of the working class—were actually of Indian origin, so it was hardly surprising that people such as M. A.

Raschid joined the movement. The minorities in the frontier areas, on the other hand, never participated in the Burmese nationalist movement; they lived in a separate political and ethnic world and eventually developed their own nationalist movements, which, at least in the beginning, wanted total separation from Burma.

Suu Kyi herself has analyzed the movement of the 1930s in her study, *Burma and India: Some Aspects of Intellectual Life under Colonialism.*[16] Comparing the different intellectual traditions of these countries, she argues that India already in the nineteenth century managed to bring new, mainly Western ideas relatively harmoniously into its development without losing its identity, whereas a much later and less widespread renaissance in Burma fell short of achieving an East-West, old-new synthesis at the intellectual level.

But there was no time to allow political attitudes to mature intellectually before World War II broke out, Suu Kyi argues.

> With the advance of the Japanese the Burmese had to face a new set of problems. They had to learn to cope with a fellow Asian race whose achievements they admired and who professed to be their allies. . . . It was against a different background from that which had prevailed under the British that the Burmese had to continue their search for a synthesis of ideas and action which would carry their nation to the required goal as an integrated whole.[17]

That search took Aung San and a number of other Burmese nationalists on a clandestine mission to Japan in 1940. Peaceful political activities on the campus of Rangoon University were no more; the young militants had decided to resort to armed struggle against the British.

Initially, Aung San and another leftist *thakin*, Hla Myaing, had been instructed to go to Shanghai to contact the Chinese Communists led by Mao Zedong. But they were in a hurry—the colonial authorities had issued a warrant for Aung San's arrest because of his political activities—so he and Hla Myaing took the first Chinese ship they could find. They disguised themselves as Chinese deck passengers Tan Luan Shung and Tan Su Taung.[18]

It was August 8, 1940, and the ship happened to be destined for Amoy (Xiamen in Pinyin transliteration)—a coastal city in China's Fujian province that was occupied by the Japanese. The Japanese tracked them down and instead of ending up with Mao Zedong's partisans in the mountains of China, Aung San and Mya Hlaing were taken to Tokyo.

The Japanese listened carefully to the two young Burmese. They were promised what they wanted—arms and military training to fight the British. The Japanese took them to Thailand, and while Hla Myaing remained behind in Bangkok, Aung San, again in disguise, returned to Rangoon in February 1941.

The following month, he left with four of his comrades. Among them was his close friend Thakin Hla Pe, or Bo Let Ya, a co-founder of the CPB. With the cooperation of the Daitoa Shipping Company—one of many fronts for Japanese intelligence—they boarded the *Shunten Maru*, bound for Tokyo.

Military training began in April with just the six of them: Mya Hlaing had returned from Thailand to join the exercises, which were held not in Japan proper but in a jungle environment on the Japanese-held Chinese island of Hainan.

In April, seven more *thakin* were also smuggled out of Burma by the Japanese on board a ship called *Kairu Maru*. That batch included Ko Aung Thein and Thakin Shwe, who were later to be known under their noms de guerre Bo Ye Htut and Bo Kyaw Zaw. In early June, three more *thakin* followed, and in July two arrived in Hainan. A Burmese drama student in Tokyo, Ko Saung, had joined the initial meeting but never participated in the actual military training in Hainan. But including him, there were now nineteen young Burmese nationalists preparing to fight for independence.

Then, in July, an unexpected fourth batch of eleven arrived on board the *Koreyu Maru*, which belonged to the same Japanese shipping line. This last group included several members of a rightist, minority faction of the Dohbama, the so-called Thakin Ba Sein–Thakin Tun Oke group. Thakin Tun Oke himself was in the last batch, accompanied by Thakin Shu Maung, who later became Bo Ne Win and Burma's military dictator from 1962 to 1988. Their arrival caused some concern among Aung San and his comrades, who belonged to the main Dohbama faction, which honored the old leftist nationalist writer Thakin Kodaw Hmaing. It was becoming evident that the Japanese did not really trust Aung San and his leftist comrades, so the Ba Sein–Tun Oke group, including Ne Win, was brought in—and their political beliefs were more in tune with Japanese fascism at the time.

Frictions soon arose between the original group and the latecomers. According to Bo Kyaw Zaw:

> Aung San and Ne Win quarreled quite often [in Hainan]. . . . Aung San was always very straightforward; Ne Win much more cunning and calculating. But Aung San's main objection to Ne Win was his immoral character. He was a gambler and a womanizer, which the strict moralist Aung San—and the rest of us as well—despised. But for the sake of unity, we kept together as much as we could.[19]

By now it was clear that the initial unity among the *thakin* belonged to the past. Various rival factions began to emerge between the leftists and the rightists. It should also be noted that the connection with Japan was not established simply because Aung San had caught the wrong ship in Rangoon. Various Japanese agents had been carrying out secret activities in Rangoon and elsewhere. In the early 1930s, a Japanese naval officer called Shozo Kokubu had made contact with the Ba Sein–Tun Oke faction. In 1940, another Burmese nationalist, Dr. Thein Maung, had visited Tokyo on a trip organized by a Japanese agent in Rangoon, Dr. Tsukasa Suzuki.[20]

However, Thakin Kodaw Hmaing's followers, among them Aung San, were suspicious of the Japanese, and the aborted trip to China should be seen as an attempt to find another source of support for their struggle for independence. When that failed, only the Japanese option was open to the young nationalists.

The Japanese were clearly aware of this, which may help explain why they decided to include the Tun Oke–Ba Sein faction in their training program. Thakin Ba Sein together with Thakin Tun Oke had begun contacting the Japanese as early as 1938. On their recommendation, Ba

Sein had already tried to cross the border to Thailand, only to be caught and imprisoned.

Whatever the motives of the Japanese, with the arrival of this last batch, the group of young nationalists had grown to thirty. Hence they became known in Burmese history as the Thirty Comrades. Their Japanese commander was Col. Keiji Suzuki, the officer who had apprehended Aung San and Mya Hlaing in Amoy. While the only guiding principle of the Thirty Comrades, regardless of faction, was independence for Burma, Col. Suzuki and Japanese intelligence had other plans in mind.

Japan had invaded eastern China, and in order to cut Allied supplies going on the Burma Road to Nationalist Chinese (Kuomintang) forces fighting the Imperial Army, the Japanese wanted an indigenous Burmese fighting force to boost their chances of success. This intelligence program was code-named "Minami Kikan," and the young Burmese in Japan unwittingly formed a vital part of it.

Aung San may also have been somewhat naive in dealing with the Japanese, and, because of his hero status in post-independent Burma, it is sometimes conveniently forgotten that even he came under the influence of totalitarianism during his sojourn in Japan. In 1941 in Tokyo, Aung San wrote:

> What we want is a strong state administration as exemplified in Germany and Italy. There shall be only one nation, one state, one party, one leader. There shall be no parliamentary opposition, no nonsense of individualism. Everyone must submit to the state which is supreme over the individual. . . . To reconstruct and maintain an independent Burma, however, is impossible unless we are strong to defend our country and protect our advance, unless we have a strong defence structure. We shall have to build powerful Army, Navy and Air Forces, and here to help the Japanese is imperative.[21]

And help they did. In December 1941, twenty-eight of the thirty comrades were transferred to Bangkok; Ko Saung, the drama student, never joined the army and one of the young Burmese, Thakin Than Tin, had succumbed to malaria in Formosa when the training in Hainan had shifted there. The Burma Independence Army (BIA), was formally set up in Bangkok on the twenty-sixth. Thakin Hla Pe, who became known as Bo Let Ya, later recalled:

> Enthusiasm ran high and each one of us drew blood from the arm to drink an oath of loyalty. That night we had a meeting of all those who had returned from the training camps in Japan, and Aung San suggested that we should each pick an auspicious name that would give pride and confidence and a sense of mission, a name to carry on our march. It was Aung San's idea and not one we conceived by collective or prolonged thinking. We liked the idea when it was put to us, and at the meeting we made our selections, tried them out, liked them, and felt a few inches taller wearing the new names.[22]

"Bo" was added to all their new noms de guerre: it was a military title that commanded respect and authority. Thus, Aung San became Bo Teza (Powerful Officer), Hla Pe assumed the name Bo Let Ya (Right Hand Officer), Aung Than was Bo Setkya (Officer of the Flying Weapon), Shu Maung became Bo Ne Win (Sun of Glory), and so on. The sole exception was Thakin Tun Oke, who assumed a Japanese name.

Col. Suzuki, the commander of the group, was named Bo Mogyo (Thunder) because the Japanese officer had wanted a Burmese name also, and his nom de guerre was given to him by Aung San. Although *mogyo* may mean "thunder," there is also a much more subtle explanation to Suzuki's Burmese name. A Burmese saying circulated during the British rule: *Htiyo-ko mogyo pyit mai*. This prophecy literally meant, "A Royal Dynasty [the British colonial power] will be struck by a bolt of lightning."[23]

In early 1942, the BIA entered Burma together with the Japanese army. Apart from the twenty-eight original members, many more Burmese joined in Thailand and along the border. On March 7, 1942, the Japanese, aided by the BIA, captured Rangoon. The British retreated to the northwest, across the border to safety in India.

The myth of European invincibility had been dispelled, which greatly encouraged the Burman nationalists to look back into history in search of their own military tradition instead of developing the more enlightened tendencies that had begun to emerge in the 1930s but had never taken firm root in Burmese thinking. This was reflected by the titles that were given to the head of state when the Japanese granted "independence" to Burma on August 1, 1943. The leader, Dr. Ba Maw, who had been a prominent politician in the 1930s, became "Naingngandaw Adipadi" (Supreme Ruler). He also assumed the title "Anashin Mingyi Kodaw" (Lord Power, the Great King's Royal Person).

After more than a decade of liberal and left-wing influences, Burma's authoritarian tradition had resurfaced in the form of Axis-sponsored *Führerschaft* with tendencies that clearly hinted at National Socialism. Ne Win became commander of the reorganized nationalist forces, now renamed the Burma National Army.

But it was wrong to assume that the Allies had given up. From bases in Assam in northeastern India, preparations began for an alternative to the Burma Road to reach out to the Chinese front once again. British and American forces, assisted by local Kachin hilltribe guerrillas, built a new road from the Indian border, through the Hukawng Valley and on to China. Fierce fighting with Japanese forces raged for more than two years before the road was completed. In the southeast, Karen and other hilltribe guerrillas also fought the Japanese invader. The Burmese nationalists retaliated by burning Karen villages, killing civilians, and raping women. Centuries-old animosity between the lowland Burmans and the highland peoples, which only *Pax Britannica* had kept in check, flared anew.

Before long, however, the Burman nationalists began to have their doubts about the real intentions of the Japanese. It was clear that the "independence" that the Japanese had granted Burma was bogus; the Japanese occupying power continued to control all aspects of life, and it also turned out to be extremely brutal in its treatment of the civilian population.

Some of their more radical ex-fellow students, now in the CPB, were already in the underground. By 1945, the entire Burmese nationalist movement turned against the Japanese and secretly contacted the Allies in India. On March 27, 1945, they eventually declared war against the

Japanese. Four months later, the red flag with a white star of the Burmese resistance flew beside the Union Jack in Rangoon. The war was over—and Burma's democratic process, interrupted by the Japanese occupation, gained momentum once again. And since then, March 27 has been celebrated officially as Armed Forces Day—a major event especially following the military takeover in 1962.

A broad-based popular front, the Anti-Fascist People's Freedom League (AFPFL), was set up by Aung San at the end of the war. In the eyes of the Burmese he had emerged as a war hero because he had journeyed to Japan to seek help for Burma's independence struggle, and then had the grace to change his mind in what he thought was the best interest of the people. Even if it actually was the British, and ethnic minority guerrillas, who had done most of the fighting against the Japanese, Aung San's BIA came to symbolize, in the eyes of the Burmese, the country's quest for freedom. The British, however, were divided in their views of the new, thirty-one-year-old national leader. Winston Churchill described Aung San in such terms as the "traitor rebel leader" of a "quisling army."[24] Author Christopher Sykes, in his biography of British wartime hero Orde Wingate, called Aung San "a jackalish youth in Japanese employ."[25]

But others, such as the returning conservative governor, Sir Reginald Dorman-Smith, realized that it would be a serious mistake not to recognize Aung San's popularity and importance for stability in postwar Burma. On leaving the restored colony in 1946, he said, "We must, I think, accept as a fact that Aung San is the most important figure in Burma today. Everyone appears to trust and admire him. . . . His troops adore him and will do anything he says. . . . He has no ambition. . . . If there were an election in Burma now and Aung San were to head a party he would sweep the country."[26]

The AFPFL became a mass movement, and Aung San and his colleagues held mass meetings throughout the country. In September 1946, the new and last governor, Sir Hubert Rance, agreed that Aung San and his party should enter as the majority in the Executive Council, which served as Burma's government. Aung San became chief councilor and de facto prime minister, and, on January 27, 1947, he signed an agreement in London with British Labour Party prime minister Clement Attlee that promised full independence for Burma within one year. Aung San did not want to repeat the mistake he had made with the Japanese and achieve only some half-hearted, sham independence. Therefore, Burma was going to become an independent republic outside the British Commonwealth, unlike India and Pakistan, which, in 1947, became dominions within the Commonwealth with the British monarch as head of state, represented by a governor-general. India later became a republic, but, even so, remained a member of the Commonwealth. Burma did not.

Aung San also had to convince the ethnic minorities to join his proposed Union of Burma. So, in February 1947, Aung San traveled to Panglong in the Shan area of northeastern Burma where he signed a second agreement, this time with leaders of the Shan, Kachin, and Chin ethnic minorities. The Shan area was not actually part of Burma proper; it was a protectorate consisting of more than thirty principalities. Ethnically the Shan are more closely related to their Thai cousins in the east than to the Burmans and the minorities that speak Tibeto-Burman languages. But they agreed to join the proposed Union of Burma if they were allowed to retain their autonomy. The Shan *saohpa* (princes) also asked for, and were granted, the right to secede from the Union after a ten-year period of independence—that is, in 1958—should they be dissatisfied with the new federation.

The day the Panglong Agreement was signed, February 12, has since then been celebrated officially in Burma as Union Day, a national holiday. A new constitution was drafted that borrowed heavily from those of Ireland, Yugoslavia, and India. It was democratic and federal in character and safeguarded basic civil liberties as well as the rights of the minorities. Totalitarianism, which had briefly resurfaced during the first stages of the Japanese occupation, was now unequivocally left behind. Or, at least, that was what most Burmese nationalists thought at the time.

While the constitution was being drafted, Aung San addressed the ethnic minorities, saying that "the Frontier Areas may or may not join the Union of Burma. There is no force and no compulsion. It is for you to make the decision freely and frankly."[27]

Seen in retrospect, it is plausible to assume that all these promises and concessions to the frontier peoples were given in order to rally the broadest possible support for a quick solution to the problems surrounding Burma's unity and independence. It is, for instance, doubtful whether the right to secede would have been granted if Burma's independence process had been somewhat slower.

Nevertheless, everything appeared set for Burma's independence when a totally unexpected event took place. On the morning of July 19, 1947, a band of gunmen burst into the Secretariat Building—the headquarters of the administration—in central Rangoon during a cabinet meeting headed by Aung San. Coldly and quickly they killed him and several others of his cabinet members who had been preparing to take over Burma after the British had left. On the same day, the Rangoon police arrested U Saw, the leader of the "Galon Force" and Aung San's main rival for the premiership of independent Burma. He was charged with murder, convicted, and hanged in May 1948.

Aung San Suu Kyi, who was born just over two months before the Japanese surrender on August 15, 1945, was only two years old when her father was assassinated. Years later, her British husband Michael Aris wrote in the introduction to a collection of her writings, "Suu . . . has only the dimmest recollections of her father. However, everything she has learned about him inclined her to believe in his selfless courage and his vision of a free and democratic Burma. Some would say she became obsessed with the image of the father she never knew."[28]

It was mainly the mother, Daw Khin Kyi, who instilled in her children a strong memory of their father.[29] In 1942, Aung San had fallen sick while fighting and was taken to Rangoon General Hospital. Doctors, nurses, and orderlies found him difficult to deal with, but one senior nurse was able not only to calm him down but also to charm him. Not long after, they were married. Two sons, Aung San U and Aung San Lin, were born, followed in 1945 by Aung San Suu Kyi. She was named "Aung San" for her father, "Suu" after her paternal grandmother, and "Kyi" after her mother. Combined, the name means "a bright collection of strange victories."[30]

The following year, Khin Kyi gave birth to another girl, who lived for only a few days. More tragedy was to follow. When Suu Kyi was seven and a half years old, her brother Aung San Lin drowned in a pond in the garden in their family home in Rangoon. Suu Kyi was devastated. She was much closer to San Lin than to her other brother, San U. It was after the death of Aung San Lin that what remained of the family moved into a new house on University Avenue, the leafy residence by Inya Lake where Suu Kyi has been under house arrest for most of the time since 1989.

Khin Kyi, now alone with two children, promoted reading at home and taught them the Buddhist values of compassion, modesty, and, especially important for Suu Kyi, honesty. There were also Christian influences in the family. As a child, Suu Kyi read the Bible; her maternal grandfather was a Christian who taught her to be open-minded about faith. Some have assumed that Aung San Suu Kyi's maternal grandfather was a Karen because he was Christian and came from Henzada, which has a large Christian Karen population. However, according to Michael Aris, he was not a Karen but a Christian Burman. Khin Kyi was a Buddhist, but she also respected Christian beliefs.[31]

Khin Kyi was not just an ordinary housewife. She became one of Burma's most outstanding public figures in her own right. She had succeeded her assassinated husband as MP for Lanmadaw constituency but resigned in 1948 to take up the post of director of the Women and Children Welfare Board, and later, chairman of the Social Planning Commission and the Council of Social Services. She was active in charities and community services.

Suu Kyi's earliest memories must have been of a land in great turmoil. Burma became an independent republic on January 4, 1948. The AFPFL's vice president, the former student leader Thakin Nu, now referred to as U Nu, became its first prime minister, and he remained in this position throughout Burma's fourteen-year-long experiment with parliamentary democracy. U Nu was a devout Buddhist and a brilliant intellectual, but he lacked Aung San's firmness and charisma. With the death of Aung San, Burma had also been robbed of the only man Burmans as well as the non-Burman nationalities trusted. Above all, the new leader, U Nu, did not control the military in the same ways Aung San had done.

The autonomous status of the army was further enhanced when the CPB went underground on March 28, two and a half months after independence. The CPB had been expelled from the AFPFL in 1946 because of personal disagreements with Aung San, and, in any case, favored a total socialist revolution instead of the parliamentary democracy that the AFPFL had created. To the communists, Burma was not independent because big British and other foreign firms still controlled much of the economy. They wanted to create a socialist people's republic and resorted to armed struggle to achieve it.

The Karen, Karenni, Mon, and Muslims in the West later took up arms against Rangoon as well. The tactical mistakes of the Burmese nationalist movement during the war—siding with the Japanese and butchering Karen and other ethnic civilians—had widened the gap between the Burmans and the various frontier peoples who were, generally speaking, more pro-British than the Burman majority.

In an attempt to forge national unity, the Shan leader Sao Shwe Thaike had been given the ceremonial post of the first president of the Union of Burma. But events in the Shan states thwarted further attempts to placate opposition among the Shan. In early 1950, several thousand Kuomintang soldiers, unable to withstand the attacks of Mao Zedong's Chinese communists who had seized power in Beijing the year before, crossed into Shan territory. Bases were set up in remote areas along the frontier, including an air base at the town of Mong Hsat near the Thai border. From these new sanctuaries in the Shan hills, the Kuomintang—with support from Chiang Kai-shek's main force in Taiwan—tried on no less than seven occasions between 1950 and 1952 to invade Yunnan, the Chinese province across the border. They were repeatedly driven back.

The Burmese army was dispatched to rid the country of these uninvited guests but was unsuccessful. U Nu then raised the question in the United Nations General Assembly, which, on April 22, 1953, adopted a resolution demanding that the Kuomintang lay down arms and leave the country.[32] Thousands of Kuomintang soldiers were evacuated by special aircraft from Lampang airport in northern Thailand with pomp and ceremony—at the same time as reinforcements were being flown in to Mong Hsat by nightly flights.

The Kuomintang invasion, combined with the government's inability to repel the uninvited guests, meant that the Shan became squeezed between two forces, both of which were perceived as foreign. When ten years' of independence was up in 1958, demands were raised for secession from the Union. When there was no response from Rangoon, bands of young Shan took to the hills to fight for independence. The war had spread to a previously tranquil and peaceful part of the country with immense human suffering as a result.

Using rebel activities and political squabbles in Rangoon as a pretext, the army commander, Gen. Ne Win, stepped in and formed a caretaker government in October 1958. Meanwhile, and because of the civil war, the strength of the armed forces had grown from 15,000 at the time of independence in 1948, to 40,000 in 1955, and more than 100,000 in 1960.[33] The army ran trading companies, its own bank, a publishing house, retail stores, a shipping line, and other businesses.[34] In the late 1950s, the Burmese military even formulated a policy that strongly resembled the *dwifungsi* (dual function) doctrine of Indonesia's army, which stated that the military had both a defense and a social-political role. A document entitled "The National Ideology and the Role of the Defence Services" spoke of regeneration, which was the result of the "decisive leadership of the government and the clarity and conviction of the Defence Services."[35] After having successfully entered business, the army, led by Gen. Ne Win, had now begun to show a more direct interest in politics and the running of the country.

While civil war was raging in parts of the countryside and the frontier areas, Suu Kyi went to school in Rangoon. Like the children of many other prominent Burmese families, she attended the Methodist English High School, one of the most prestigious and strictest in the country. She was a bright pupil and especially good at languages. U Ohn, a former ambassador to the Soviet Union and the United Kingdom, was a close associate of the family and, when visiting Rangoon, he always brought back books for her. Suu Kyi was brought up reading not only Burmese and Buddhist literature but also books on Greek mythology and European classics, verse as well as prose.

Then, in 1960, Khin Kyi was appointed Burma's ambassador to India. The son, Aung San U, went to England to study engineering, and never returned to Asia except on occasional visits. He later settled in San Diego, California.

Suu Kyi, however, followed her mother to New Delhi. She was fifteen when they arrived there, an impressionable age in anybody's life. It was during her teenage years in India that she acquired her lasting admiration for the principles of nonviolence embodied in the life and philosophy of Mahatma Gandhi.[36] Buddhist monks from Burma, Thailand, and Cambodia were frequent guests at the residence of the Burmese ambassador in New Delhi. The prime minister of India at the time, Jawaharlal Nehru, had been an acquaintance of Aung San, so it was not surprising that Suu Kyi made friends with his grandsons, Rajiv and Sanjay Gandhi.[37]

Suu Kyi completed her schooling in New Delhi, first at high school and later at Lady Shri Ram College, where she was always top of her class. While in India she also took piano lessons and a course in ikebana, or Japanese flower arrangement. She was described as a serious young woman, quiet and correct, and she remained in the background when her mother entertained visitors at the embassy and their home.[38]

While Khin Kyi and Suu Kyi were in New Delhi, momentous events were taking place back in Burma. On March 1, 1962, a visiting Chinese ballet troupe staged a performance in Rangoon. It attracted a large audience, among whom could be seen the increasingly powerful Gen. Ne Win. The show went on until late in the evening. When it was over, the general shook the hand of the leading Chinese ballerina and then quietly left. The audience assumed that he was going home to sleep after watching the show.

But the general had other plans. U Nu had returned as prime minister following elections in 1960 and the dissolution of Ne Win's caretaker government. One of U Nu's most pressing tasks was to find a solution to Burma's ethnic crisis, and in order to do so he had convened a Nationalities' Seminar in Rangoon that was attended by Shan and Karenni representatives.

In the early hours of March 2, troops moved in to take over strategic positions in the capital. Under the cover of darkness, U Nu, five other ministers, the chief justice, and over thirty Shan and Karenni leaders were taken into custody. Among them was ex-president Sao Shwe Thaike, who was led away by soldiers, never to be seen again. Another prominent Shan leader, the Hsipaw *saohpa* Sao Kya Seng was stopped at a roadblock near the Shan state capital of Taunggyi. He had flown there to visit his sister after having attended the parliament in Rangoon. He also disappeared, and not even his relatives know what happened to him.[39]

There was no bloodshed in Rangoon on the actual day of the coup, apart from a shootout at Sao Shwe Thaike's house on Kokine Road. His seventeen-year-old son Sai Myee was gunned down by the raiding soldiers on the night Ne Win seized power.

The following day, the constitution was suspended and the parliament dissolved. A twenty-four-member Revolutionary Council headed by Ne Win took over and began to rule by decree. The "ideology" of the new regime was published shortly after the coup in a document entitled "The Burmese Way to Socialism." This was followed later by "The System of Correlation of Man and His Environment," which again was an effort to provide philosophical underpinnings for the military government. It was a hodgepodge of Marxism, Buddhist thinking, and humanism that reflected an attempt by Ne Win to give his regime a semblance of belonging to Burma's specific political traditions.[40]

In reality, however, Burma went into a state of self-imposed isolation, and the economy deteriorated to a point of near-bankruptcy. All banks and private enterprises were nationalized, and Burma's previously free press was strangled. All political organizations, except the newly established Burma Socialist Programme Party (BSPP), and its offshoots, were banned.

It was a curious type of socialism that was introduced. State corporations run by the military took over the production, distribution, and sale of everything imaginable. By adding the word "people" in front of the new enterprises and organs of state control, the military tried to give its rule an air of real socialism, which they hoped would appeal to the "masses." Beer and alcoholic drinks came from "The People's Brewery and Distillery." Fashion-conscious ladies had their hair done at "The People's Pride Hairdressing Salon." The public was supposedly protected by "The

People's Police Force" and ruled by a number of "People's Councils" on different levels, while the judiciary was renamed the "Council of People's Justices." And, neatest of them all, pastries were sold by "The People's Patisseries," while toothpaste came from "The People's Toilet Industry."

The dark era of Burmese history had begun. Ne Win, being one of the Thirty Comrades, claimed to have inherited the mantle of leadership from Aung San, although there was little in the new policies that continued the traditions of Burma's independence hero.

This fact is often overlooked, primarily by Burmese scholars, and few countries in the modern world have in recent times been victim of so many misrepresentations as Burma. These have ranged from a glossy guidebook image of Burma as a land of smiling people and golden pagodas to apparently serious attempts by some writers to give successive repressive regimes since 1962 an air of respectability by perpetuating the myth that they were the logical consequence of Burmese traditions.

The essence of this theory is that Burma has always been an authoritarian state with a strong center. Therefore, the colonial era with its nineteenth- and twentieth-century liberalism, and its extension during the democratic period immediately after independence, were little more than brief, alien interludes in the country's history. Following the military takeover in 1962, the Burmese state "reasserted" the continuity that the colonials and liberals had upset. True, Burma has had an authoritarian past, but it also has a strong intellectual and creative tradition. And it is questionable how far beyond the court the kings' authoritarian rule ever actually reached.

Apart from apologists for Ne Win and the regimes that succeeded his, there is no one who believes that there was any strong and well-organized "Burmese state" before the British colonized the country in the nineteenth century and created its present boundaries. Pre-colonial Burma was ruled by warrior kings who were adept at conquering land from their neighbors, including parts of what today is Thailand, but they failed to consolidate their conquests by establishing functioning administrations in their new acquisitions. Consequently, Burmese kingdoms rose and fell with a certain ruler. That warrior-king mentality, not any ancient notion of a "Burmese state," is the main legacy of "old

Burma" and is the reason why the country even today is fractured and in a permanent state of civil war.

Another myth is that the 1962 takeover was "bloodless." Apart from Sai Myee and the Shan leaders who disappeared in March, there was a bloody massacre at Rangoon University in July. When Ne Win first seized power, there was disbelief and many did not know what to make of it. People remembered the 1958–60 Caretaker Government and thought that the military just wanted to restore order and then hand back power to a civilian government. But when fundamental changes began to occur, people—especially students—began to protest.

On July 7, 1962, thousands of students gathered at the campus in Rangoon, declaring it a "fortress of democracy." All day, speeches were given condemning the coup and calling for the restoration of democracy. The Students' Union building, which had been an important symbol of Burmese nationalism since the 1930s, was alive with activities and filled with youthful laughter and cheerful bantering.

Then the soldiers arrived. Bullets began to fly—right into the crowd. It was clear that the soldiers were under orders to shoot to kill.[41] The man in charge of the operation was Sein Lwin, one of Ne Win's closest lieutenants, who previously had distinguished himself by hunting down and killing the charismatic Karen rebel leader Saw Ba U Gyi in a hideout near the Thai border in 1950.

Officially, fifteen were killed and twenty-seven wounded. But both neutral observers and students who were present during the shooting say that the university looked like a slaughterhouse where not fifteen but hundreds of potential leaders of society in many fields lay sprawled in death.

In the early hours of July 8, Rangoon residents were awakened by an explosion that reverberated through the city. The army had dynamited the historic Students' Union building, reducing it to rubble.

Suu Kyi left India for Britain in 1964 to further her studies at St. Hugh's College in Oxford. Three years later, she earned a BA in philosophy, politics, and economics and worked for a while as a research assistant at the School of Oriental and African Studies at the University of London. Her hosts and sponsors in Britain were Sir Paul, later Lord, Gore-Booth, a former British ambassador to Burma and High Commissioner to India, and his wife, Patricia. Sir Paul acted as her guardian when he was permanent under-secretary at the Foreign and Commonwealth Office in London. Through the Gore-Booth family, she met Michael Aris, a student of Tibetology, whom she was later to marry.

During the turmoil of 1988–89, some of her political rivals—among them the NLD's first, disgraced leader, Aung Gyi, and his close associate, a veteran journalist called Sein Win—told nearly every visiting foreign journalist in Burma that Suu Kyi during her time at St. Hugh's was deeply involved in "radical student politics."[42] Her friends from that time paint an entirely different picture of her. There is no record of her being involved in any political activities as a student. Unlike Pakistan's Benazir Bhutto, who served as president of the Students' Union at Oxford, Suu Kyi was not politically active while in Britain. She devoted her energies to contributing academic papers to various seminars on South and Southeast Asian culture. One of many friends in Oxford was Sunethra Bandaranaike, the daughter of the late Sri Lankan leader S. W. R. D. Bandaranaike. Other friends included Indians who shared her deep interest in British as well as Asian cultures. At Oxford she was also close to Ann Pasternak, the niece of dissident Soviet writer Boris Pasternak.[43]

Throughout her time abroad she continued to visit Burma regularly. She maintained her Burmese citizenship, and old fellow students remember how even in Oxford she dressed in traditional Burmese clothing. Nalini Jain, now a lecturer at the English department of the National University of Singapore, studied at Oxford at the same time as Suu Kyi, and later became her neighbor. She recalls, "For all the long years that she spent in the west, hers was the *sarong* or *longyi*-clad figure that cycled down the High Street. And she was brought up with grit and discipline. She never slouched and always stood up to situations and events."[44]

Suu Kyi, however, never fully completed her studies and left in 1969 to work for the Advisory Committee on Administrative and Budgetary Questions at the UN Secretariat in New York. This was at the time when U Thant served as secretary general of the UN, and he had attracted a small crowd of Burmese to New York. Suu Kyi shared a small apartment in midtown Manhattan with Dora Than E, a close family friend who had been a famous singer in Burma before the war. Suu Kyi usually referred to Dora Than E, who worked as a UN information officer in the 1970s, as her "emergency aunt." There was always Burmese food at home, the two women spoke Burmese to each other, and their apartment was known as "a Burmese home in Manhattan." In her free time from the UN she worked as a volunteer social worker at Bellevue Hospital in New York. Her main intellectual inspiration during this time came from the civil rights movement which then was sweeping through the United States. In Martin Luther King's speeches she found similarities with the ideals of Mahatma Gandhi, with which she was already keenly familiar.

In an interview with a representative of Amnesty International published in July 1989, Suu Kyi reiterated that the NLD did "not want violence" but at the same time said that the league's commitment to nonviolence did "not mean we are going to sit back weakly and do nothing." She also said that "civil disobedience has a great history" and pointed out that she had recently begun putting forward Mahatma Gandhi and Martin Luther King as models in her speeches.[45]

She was separated from her close friend Michael Aris, who had been employed since 1967 as private tutor to the royal family of the Himalayan kingdom of Bhutan and as head of the Translation Department in the capital Thimphu. But they wrote letters to each other, and love developed. She visited him in Bhutan in 1971. Michael remembers this time as one of the happiest in his life. They rode on horseback and trekked in Bhutan's spectacular mountains and green valleys. They became engaged.[46]

On New Year's Day 1972, Suu Kyi and Michael were married in a simple Burmese-style ceremony at the Gore-Booths' house in London. Her time in Britain and her marriage to an Englishman are perhaps the most controversial aspects of her life. Many Burmese perceive interracial marriages as a rejection of their culture and the traditions of "Burmeseness." On the other hand, given the nature of the male-dominated Burmese society, it is doubtful whether a Burmese husband would have allowed her to develop her talents as independently as she did. And it was clear already at this time that she felt she had inherited from her father an obligation to her country.

According to Michael Aris:

> She always used to say to me that if her people ever needed her, she would not fail them. Recently I read again the 187 letters she sent to me in Bhutan from New York in the eight months before we married in London on January 1, 1972. Again and again she expressed her worry that her family and people might misinterpret our marriage and see it as a lessening of her devotion to them. She constantly reminded me that one day she would have to return to Burma, that she counted on my support at that time, not as her due, but as a favour.[47]

Suu Kyi, on her part, told Michael:

> I only ask one thing, that should my people need me, you would help me do my duty by them. Would you mind very much should such a situation arise? How probable is it I do not know, but the possibility is there. Sometimes I am beset by fears that circumstances might tear us apart just when we are so happy in each other that separation would be a torment. And yet such fears are so futile and inconsequential: if we love and cherish each other as much as we can while we can, I am sure love and compassion will triumph in the end.[48]

The need for someone to emerge as an opponent to Ne Win's military regime in Rangoon was becoming urgent, as Burma's economy continued to deteriorate, and there were signs of growing discontent with the new order. In May 1974, the oil workers in Chauk, west of Mandalay, went on strike demanding higher wages. The unrest spread from the oil fields to Rangoon, where railway workers and laborers at a spinning mill also laid down their tools. Ne Win responded as he had done when the students had demonstrated in 1962: he sent in troops who fired indiscriminately into the crowds. Officially, twenty-eight were killed and eighty wounded. Independent sources put the death toll at about one hundred. Hundreds were arrested, and universities and colleges were closed because the students had demonstrated their support for the striking workers.

More unrest occurred in December 1974. U Thant, the secretary general of the United Nations, had died in New York on November 25. He was the internationally best-known and most respected Burmese citizen, but stood for everything that Burma's military government was not. He was a brilliant statesman and intellectual, well-educated and articulate, and not a supporter of military dictatorships.

When his body was flown back to Rangoon, the authorities planned to bury it in an obscure cemetery on the outskirts of the capital. The students, almost inevitably, seized the opportunity to launch anti-military demonstrations. As the funeral procession moved towards the burial site, a group of students snatched the coffin and carried it away to the university campus. Buddhist monks joined them, and the students buried U Thant on the old site of the Students' Union building, which the army had dynamited in 1962. The students and monks shouted "Down with the fascist government!" and "Down with the one-party dictatorship!"

The response from the government was perhaps predictable. It sent out its troops again. The campus was occupied, and the coffin with U Thant's remains was seized and later reburied near the Shwe Dagon Pagoda. Martial law was declared on December 11, and when student demonstrators defied the curfew, the soldiers opened fire. The official casualty toll was once again ludicrously low: nine killed and seventy-four wounded. Students who participated in the demonstrations assert that hundreds of their comrades were gunned down that day in Rangoon. The government blamed the unrest on "unscrupulous elements from the outside who have created disturbances" and made vague references to communist influences. No attempt was made to understand the deeper causes of resentment with the military authorities and the BSPP dictatorship.[49]

Scores of students and other activists fled to the Thai border, where U Nu, Bo Let Ya, and some other pre-coup leaders were organizing armed resistance to the regime. They were based in areas controlled by the Karen National Union (KNU), and supported by other ethnic rebel armies, as well. But it was a rather unusual rebel movement. The collapse of the Burmese economy following the introduction of the "Burmese Way to Socialism" had led to a flourishing black-market trade in consumer goods and other daily necessities from Thailand to Burma, with timber, precious stones, minerals, and other raw materials flowing the other way. The KNU and other border-based ethnic rebel armies set up a series of "toll gates" through which the contraband was funneled. In this way, the rebels were able to buy weapons on the black market in Thailand.

In the opium-growing areas in Shan State, drugs became a medium of exchange that benefited the rebels and the government alike. The rebels traded in, or just taxed, opium to sustain their armies. In order to fight the rebels, the government had in 1963 authorized the setting up of local home guard armies called "Ka Kwe Ye" (KKY). These militia units were given the right to use all government-controlled roads and towns in Shan State for opium smuggling in exchange for combating the rebels.[50]

There were three reasons for this unusual move. The first was insufficient funds in the state treasury. Rangoon could not afford to provide the KKY with money, rations, uniforms, arms, and other necessities. By trading in opium, the central government had hoped that the home guards would be self-supporting.[51] But it was also an attempt to undermine the financial basis of the Shan rebels. If the KKY could drive the insurgents out of the opium market, they would have no money to buy guns and ammunition to carry out their struggle. A third reason was the acute shortage of consumer goods that the Burmese Way to Socialism had created. The government had to turn a blind eye to the smuggling activities along Burma's borders, given the choice of contraband or no goods at all, which could result in further political and social unrest.

The KKY commanders carried their opium to the market town of Tachilek, near the border junction of Burma, Laos, and Thailand. There the opium was exchanged for bars of pure gold—and the area soon became known as the "Golden Triangle"—and consumer goods were brought back as a return cargo in their trucks and mule trains. Some of it, especially fancy furniture, was reportedly given to Burmese army officers to soften their possible disapproval of the trade.[52]

The most notorious KKY commanders were Lo Hsing-han (Luo Xinghan in Pinyin), who led the home guards in the opium-growing district of Kokang in the northeasternmost corner of Shan State, and his rival Zhang Qifu, who became known—and feared—as Khun Sa, the Lord of the Golden Triangle. Although he later claimed to be a Shan nationalist leader, he began his career as commander of the home guard unit at Loi Maw near the garrison town of Tang-yan in central Shan State. He was half-Chinese, while Lo was a pure ethnic Chinese from Kokang.

There was no shortage of opium in Shan State. At Burma's independence in 1948, the total opium production in the country totaled some thirty tons. The Kuomintang invasion and the civil war had changed all that. Opium had become the most important hard currency for all sides involved in the conflict, and production skyrocketed. Thirty years after independence, more than 400 tons of opium were harvested in northeastern Burma annually.

Suu Kyi, meanwhile, had joined her husband Michael in Bhutan, where she took the post of Research Officer in the Bhutanese Ministry of Foreign Affairs with specific responsibility for advising the foreign minister on UN affairs. They stayed in the Himalayan kingdom for two years, returning to England in 1973. There, on April 12, 1973, Suu Kyi gave birth to their first son, Alexander, who was also given the Burmese name Myint San Aung. A second son, Kim, or Htein Lin, was born in 1977. The family moved into a house in Park Town, an old and prestigious area in Oxford. Michael by then had published a scholarly work on Bhutan and was a fellow at Wolfson College. Suu Kyi took her children to school on the back of her bicycle. Their Singaporean neighbor Nalini Jain remembers: "Often when I think of Suu I recall a figure on a bicycle. For till this day the couple never owned a car. And they never had a television set in their home."[53]

Jain also remembers Suu Kyi "as a disciplinarian mother. The children had to eat what was given them for meals and no fuss was tolerated. I remember Michael telling me, 'now if you put a snake before them, they will eat it up.' I cannot imagine Alexander and Kim lolling before a TV set. Suu brought them up as she herself had been brought up."[54] According to Jain, determination and grit have always been part of Suu Kyi's character.

Though Suu Kyi had spent years in relative luxury in her mother's ambassadorial home in New Delhi, Khin Kyi had also been a strict disciplinarian who did not tolerate extravagant lifestyles. In Oxford, Suu Kyi not only coped with all the housework, but often did it with

Kim slung on her back, Jain later recalled. She also remembers how Suu Kyi and Boris Pasternak's niece, Ann, would sometimes cycle down the streets of Oxford, Ann with her little girl Nina and Suu with Kim or Alexander. "It was a merry scene then: Ann talked to Nina in Russian, Suu chatted to her children in Burmese, and the children spoke to each other in English."[55]

By the beginning of the 1980s, after having been married for more than ten years, Aung San Suu Kyi decided to go back to academic life. While raising her sons, she undertook some teaching and research in Burmese studies. The outcome was a monograph on her father that was published in 1984 in the Leaders of Asia Series by the University of Queensland in Australia.[56] She also wrote a children's guidebook to Burma titled *Let's Visit Burma*.[57] It was written in simple language but revealed a deep devotion to the country she had left when she was a teenager.

In the following year, she was invited as a visiting scholar to the Center for Southeast Asian Studies at Kyoto University in Japan to look at Burmese material from World War II and especially documents related to her father and the Thirty Comrades. One of her main purposes was also to interview those in Japan who remembered her father. She also learnt Japanese—as did her son Kim, who accompanied her to Kyoto.

Her time in Kyoto proved important for her intellectual development. Being on her own and studying her father's work, she came to realize more profoundly who she was. She and Kim went back to Burma after completing her studies in Kyoto, and then, in 1986, to Simla, a hill station on the slopes of the Indian Himalayas, where they were joined by Michael and Alexander. Her husband had been admitted as a fellow at the Indian Institute of Advanced Study in Simla at the same time as she had gone to Kyoto. Now, she was offered and accepted a similar fellowship to prepare a manuscript comparing Burmese and Indian nationalism in the inter-war years. That was when she wrote *Burma and India: Some Aspects of Intellectual Life under Colonialism*, which, however, was not published until June 1990.[58]

She had just started a postgraduate thesis at the School of Oriental and African Studies in London when, in April 1988, her mother,

Khin Kyi, suffered a stroke. Suu Kyi immediately returned to Rangoon to look after her. For nearly four months, she tended her mother in hospital, residing there herself. She just managed to bring Khin Kyi to the family home on University Avenue when Michael, Alexander, and Kim arrived in late July—and Burma exploded.

CHAPTER 2

THE NLD: MOVEMENT, NOT PARTY

At 8:08 a.m. on August 8, 1988 (8.8.88), the dockworkers in Rangoon port walked out. That was the auspicious moment, and as soon as the word spread that the strike was on, people began marching towards the city center. Peter Conard, a Bangkok-based Buddhist scholar, happened to be in Rangoon that day. He was staying at the Dagon Hotel on Sule Pagoda Road, near the old colonial-style Globe Cinema.

> I was standing on the balcony of my hotel room just before nine a.m. when I spotted some masked youths on bicycles racing down the still almost empty roads, calling out something in Burmese. Apparently they were calling out that the demonstrators were coming. A few minutes later, some students came and formed human chains around the soldiers who were posted at main intersections. I was told the students intended to protect the troops from possibly violent demonstrators. And then the first marchers arrived. I saw them coming in a massive column across the railway bridge on Sule Pagoda Road with flags and banners heading for the city centre. There were thousands of them, clenching their fists and chanting anti-government slogans. People came out of their houses, applauding and cheering the demonstrators on.[1]

Soon, various groups of marchers appeared from all directions and everybody seemed to be on their way to the City Hall and the nearby

Bandoola Square in central Rangoon. There were young and old men, women and children, Burmans, Indians, Chinese, and people from nearly every other ethnic group in the country. They were carrying flags, banners, and portraits of the national hero Aung San. Strikingly evident was a column of hundreds of Buddhist monks carrying their alms bowls upside down to indicate that the nation was on strike. Within an hour, the entire city center was solidly packed with tens of thousands of people. The balconies of the surrounding houses were crammed with spectators, and some even went up to the rooftops. About ten makeshift podiums were erected outside the City Hall, and one speaker after another went up to denounce the government. It was a clear and sunny day.

"We want democracy! Down with the government! Down with Sein Lwin!" the crowd chanted, tens-of-thousands strong. Street vendors handed out cheroots, sweets, bread, and snacks to the demonstrators, and people stuck wads of banknotes into the hands of those who seemed to be the organizers. A few foreign journalists who had managed to sneak into the country on tourist visas were cheered when they raised their cameras to take pictures of the marchers. Placards in English were turned in their direction while the demonstrators called out, also in English, "Let the world know that Burma has risen against the tyranny! We want democracy! Welcome, foreign journalists!"

The festive mood prevailed all day, and the army remained in the background, protected by rings of students. Spontaneously, some demonstrators struck up the national anthem, the army song, and shouted: "The *pyithu tatmadaw* (people's army) is our army!" The soldiers were addressed as *akogyi* (elder brother), as there was a widespread belief that the soldiers would join the uprising and help overthrow the government. To show the soldiers that they would have to kill their own people if they did not join them, some young demonstrators even walked up to the lines of troops that were positioned here and there, unbuttoned their shirts, and shouted: "Shoot me if you dare!"[2]

"But it was also easy to see the psychological isolation of the soldiers," Conard remembers. "Nervously clutching their automatic rifles, they seemed swamped in the sea of people and taken aback by the massive demonstrations."

The Associated Press reported:

> Marching behind red flags, symbolizing courage, and waving portraits of 1940s national hero Aung San, young students, women, monks, and other Rangoon residents . . . called for democracy and economic reform. "You couldn't see the end of it," said twenty-two-year-old British student Georgina Allen. She saw "solid flanks of organized, unarmed demonstrators clenching their fists, cheering, and clapping their hands as they marched along a main street in Rangoon."[3]

The massive demonstrations were by no means confined to Rangoon. In nearly every town across the country—Mandalay, Sagaing, and Shwebo in the north; the oil towns of Yenangyaung and Chauk along the Irrawaddy River; Bassein and Henzada in the Irrawaddy delta; Pegu, Toungoo, Pyinmana, and Minbu in the central plains; Moulmein, Mergui, and Tavoy in the southeast; Taunggyi in Shan State; and even as far north as the Kachin State capital of Myitkyina—masses of people took to the streets to vent twenty-six years of pent-up frustrations with the Burma Socialist Programme Party (BSPP) regime, which, in essence, was a military dictatorship.

Min Win Htut, a twenty-year-old chemistry student, participated in the demonstrations in the southeastern port city of Moulmein. "About one hundred thousand people gathered outside the Kyaiktouk Pagoda in the morning. There were students, monks, and ordinary people. Peasants from the countryside had arrived in lorries and bullock-carts to participate in the demonstrations. We marched through the city to the Maidan grounds." For the first time, the slogan *Dimokresi apyei-awa ya shiye do-a-ye! do-a-ye!* (We want full democracy, that's what we want!) reverberated between the walls of the old colonial-style houses in Moulmein. Columns of local Mon people, brandishing their own banners, mixed with the Burmans in a unique display of solidarity between two of the country's main ethnic groups.

However, in central Rangoon the military showed some kind of reaction. At about 5:30 p.m., Brig.-Gen. Myo Nyunt, the Rangoon commander, appeared on the portico of the City Hall along with several other high-ranking army officers. Over a loudspeaker, he firmly told the people to disperse, or the troops would open fire. Across the street on a balcony was Hmwe Hmwe, a twenty-five-year-old woman. "But nobody reacted in the way that the military had expected. The crowds only grew bigger and bigger. Myo Nyunt repeated this threat twice after the first announcement, and each time his voice seemed to be getting weaker as the demonstrators responded in unison, 'This is a peaceful demonstration! Be disciplined! No provocations!'"[4]

The euphoric atmosphere prevailed all day. In the evening, thousands of people moved to the Shwe Dagon Pagoda, where a meeting was being held. Meanwhile, Bren gun carriers and trucks full of armed soldiers were parked in the compound of the City Hall and in nearby Barr Street. But nobody really thought that the troops would be called out. "We almost thought we'd won and that the government had given up," said Ko Lin, a medical student who was out in the streets of Rangoon that day.

At 11 p.m. there were still thousands of people outside the Sule Pagoda in central Rangoon. At 11:30 p.m., trucks loaded with troops roared out from behind the nearby City Hall. These were followed by more trucks and by Bren carriers, their machine guns pointed straight in front of them. Spontaneously, the demonstrators began singing the national anthem. Two pistol shots rang out—and then the sound of machine-gun fire reverberated between the buildings surrounding Bandoola Square. People fell in droves as they were hit. The streets turned red with blood as people "scattered screaming into alleys and doorways, stumbling over open gutters, crouching by walls and then, in a new wave of panic, running again," *New York Times* reporter Seth Mydans wrote.[5]

Almost simultaneously, trucks loaded with soldiers pulled up close to a column of about two thousand people who had gathered on Shwegondine Road northwest of the Shwe Dagon Pagoda. Ko Lin, the medical student, was there.

> Some soldiers got down from the trucks and aimed their rifles towards the crowd, while others stayed on the trucks. They fired on automatic right into the thickest part of the crowd. We ran for our lives. Two young men in front of me fell to the ground and died instantly. My friend next

> to me was hit in his leg and I helped him along. People ran for cover in all directions as bullets flew through the air. We reached our house safely, but my friend was too scared to go to hospital; we treated him at home the best we could. Luckily, he survived.[6]

Richard Gourley, who was in Rangoon on that fateful day, wrote in the *Financial Times*, "Eyewitnesses saw armoured cars driving up to groups of demonstrators and opening fire indiscriminately, challenging official claims that they were using only moderate force. Some witnesses reported seeing demonstrators carrying bodies of dead protesters over their heads as they marched through the streets."[7]

Nobody knows how many people were killed that night, but the shooting continued until about three in the morning. Sit Naing, another medical student who participated in the 8.8.88 demonstrations, went to Rangoon General Hospital (RGH) as soon as he heard that the army had opened fire on the demonstrators. "I thought they needed volunteers. But that night, only two wounded were brought to RGH. They came from Shwegondine and were twins. One of them died immediately. We heard that the army was picking up dead bodies outside the Sule Pagoda and taking them away. I have no idea where."[8]

James Coles, an Australian tourist from Sydney, told Reuters on his arrival in Bangkok that he had given a lift in his hired car to a young demonstrator that night. With tears in his eyes, the young man produced two cartridges from his *longyi* and said he had picked them up at a spot where four of his colleagues had been shot when the army smashed one of the many scattered marches round the city.[9]

Shooting also occurred in the northern town of Sagaing on August 9. Two frequent visitors from Japan were in the area when the local police opened fire on demonstrators. "On that day, students were marching towards the police station in Sagaing to demand the release of other students who were being detained there. The demonstrators were joined by a large number of peasants from surrounding villages. By the time they reached the police station, the crowd had swelled to about ten thousand."[10]

At the police station, someone in the crowd—believed by local people to have been an agent provocateur—threw stones at the police, who responded with gunfire. When a male student stood up to urge the crowd not to react violently, he was immediately shot and killed. A Buddhist monk repeated the student's plea. Five bullets hit him before he died and fell to the ground. "When the monk fell, a female student shouted, 'Be calm! We're not afraid to die!' " She was shot as well.

There was a moment's silence and then an automatic gun fired into the crowd. The man who was blasting away with his Sten gun was Thura Kyaw Zwa, the Chairman of the Sagaing Division's People's Council. Hundreds of people were hit.

Another witness to the massacre in Sagaing was a fifty-three-year-old man from Manchester who was then teaching at the Mandalay Teachers' Training College. In an interview with the *Times* of London on September 23, he related the incident that had taken place more than a month before. "Two to three hundred died on the spot, others died in hospitals and elsewhere. Two weeks later, I asked a doctor who was involved how many wounded he was still treating. He said one hundred, many with hideous wounds. Most of the wounds had been inflicted from behind as the crowd rushed away."[11]

The two visitors from Japan claim that the police threw bodies into the Irrawaddy River to destroy the evidence. "Some of the injured managed to swim to safety and to report the massacre. All locals know that anything thrown in the river from the Mandalay side will float all the way downstream. But from the Sagaing side, because of a bend in the river, objects will get caught on Naukchinkyun Island a few miles away. Sure enough, bodies began washing up there soon after."

The title "thura" in front of Kyaw Zwa's name means "hero"—a distinction he had earned when he was an army lieutenant fighting communist insurgents in upper Burma. Local people in Sagaing say that he used to kill even small children, arguing that they were the "seeds of communism." Thura Kyaw Zwa was but the most extreme example of brutal autocratic army and ex-army officers who filled the posts of the BSPP administration out in the states and divisions—and who are still ruling Burma under a different guise. The state-run Burma Broadcasting Service described the incident in Sagaing on August 9 as an attack by five thousand demonstrators against the town's police station: "In order to prevent the police station from falling into the hands of the mobs, shots were fired. It is learnt that thirty-one people were killed and thirty-seven others wounded in the incident."[12]

The demonstrations continued in Rangoon, and in some parts of the city people fought back with swords, clubs, Molotov cocktails, and whatever they could grab. But they were no match for the government's well-equipped soldiers. The worst day was Wednesday, August 10. Army trucks dumped both dead and wounded from all over Rangoon outside the RGH. Some young people had a bullet wound in their arms or legs—and then a bayonet gash in their throats or chests. Several were male and stark naked—with shaven heads. Those were the monks whom the soldiers had stripped of their robes. Sit Naing, the medical volunteer, counted 160 dead and hundreds of wounded at RGH alone, and there were many other hospitals throughout Rangoon. He believes at least 1,000 people were killed in Rangoon during the period August 8–12, and more in cities and towns across the country.

A US State Department human rights report later described what happened in Rangoon between August 8 and 13:

> Numerous eyewitnesses confirm that troops clashed with and killed fleeing demonstrators and fired indiscriminately at onlookers and into houses. On 10 August, troops fired into a group of doctors and nurses, and others in front of Rangoon General Hospital . . . who were pleading with the troops to stop shooting. . . . Four separate eyewitness accounts of an August 10 incident in North Okkalapa, a working-class suburb of Rangoon, describe how soldiers knelt in formation and fired repeatedly at demonstrators in response to an army captain's orders. The first casualties were five or six teenage girls who carried flags and portraits of Burma's assassinated founding father, Aung San. All four eyewitnesses reported large numbers of dead and wounded and estimated several hundred casualties at the scene. Eyewitnesses reported similar incidents throughout Rangoon during the 8 to 13 August period. Deaths probably numbered over two thousand, but actual numbers can never be known. In many cases as soon as they finished firing, troops carted off victims for surreptitious disposal to mask the extent of the carnage.[13]

In the hospital shooting, two female and one male nurse were severely wounded, two others only slightly hurt. Several civilians—blood donors and relatives looking for their kin—were killed. News about the hospital shooting spread all over Rangoon. The very thought of shooting hospital staff, whose duty is to save lives, was horrendous and the public was further inflamed. Small, makeshift shrines of flowers, wreaths, and monks' umbrellas were erected in the hospital compound.[14]

On the eleventh, Peter Conard visited the RGH:

> Everyone was outraged. The staff had carefully circled the bullet marks on the walls with white chalk. There were also lots of posters pasted on the walls, denouncing the regime and the killings. Inside, the wards were full of wounded people, who were being treated with whatever was left of the almost depleted stocks of medicines. But we were also told that many people didn't dare bring their wounded relatives to hospital for fear of being arrested, or registered by the military. Many died in their homes, without medical care.

The massacres and street fighting eventually came to an end. When the people listened to the government radio station on Friday night, August 12, the announcer read out a brief message saying that Sein Lwin, the "Butcher of Rangoon," had resigned.

Within minutes, people were streaming out of their houses, embracing each other, laughing with tears in their eyes and dancing down the streets. Inside, housewives banged pots and pans in their kitchens; it was a night of joy after five bloody days in Rangoon.

The authorities had probably realized that the hardline approach had failed. A supposed "moderate," Dr. Maung Maung, was appointed as Burma's new president and BSPP chairman. He was a partly Western-educated academic and a prolific writer, but also a diehard Ne Win loyalist. Among his books was a flattering biography of the old strongman.[15]

But that did not placate the protesters, who felt they had won at least a partial victory. A new general strike was proclaimed and the country ground to a halt. In every city, town, and major village from Myitkyina in the north, down to Kawthaung, or Victoria Point, at the southernmost tip of Burma, millions of people marched in daily mass demonstrations on a scale that had never been seen in Southeast Asia before. And, somewhat puzzlingly for many, the army withdrew from the streets and returned to the barracks. On August 24, martial law—which had been in force since August 3—was lifted in Rangoon and Prome.

Aung San Suu Kyi had by then made her first public appearance outside the Shwe Dagon Pagoda, and emerged as the main symbol of the growing pro-democracy movement. One by one, several ex-politicians and other critics of the regime also began appearing in public and issuing statements. Aung Gyi, who to some extent had initiated the movement by his series of open letters to Ne Win the year before, became more active. Another was Tin U, the former minister of defense who had been dismissed and jailed in 1976. About 4,000 people listened to his first speech outside RGH on August 27. He quoted Dr. Maung Maung's old thesis from the 1950s, "Democracy calls for 'justice, liberty, and equality' which are the eternal principles of the [1947] constitution. That's what our president wrote thirty years ago. But now I don't know what's happened to that man."[16] The crowd roared with laughter.

Former prime minister U Nu, who had returned to Burma during a 1980 amnesty, also became active, proclaiming his own interim government on September 9. "I'm still the legitimate prime minister," the octogenarian U Nu proclaimed at a press conference in Rangoon.[17]

Even Ne Win's old comrades deserted him. On September 6, nine out of eleven survivors of the legendary Thirty Comrades called on the army to back the uprising. Only one of them, wartime hero Kyaw Zaw, could not join the appeal because he had in the 1970s left Rangoon to join the communist rebels in the hills of northeastern Shan State.[18]

All over the country people formed strike centers consisting of Buddhist monks, community elders, and even students, who took over from the BSPP-run administration, which seemed to have collapsed. Buddhist monks organized day-to-day affairs like rubbish collection, made sure the water supply was working, and, according to some reports, even acted as traffic policemen. The maintenance of law and order was also in the hands of the monks—and the criminals who had been caught were often given rather unorthodox sentences. One visitor to Mandalay in August saw a man chained to a lamp post outside the railway station who shouted all day, "I'm a thief! I'm a thief!"

The absence of policemen and soldiers in the streets of Rangoon and elsewhere also made the demonstrators more daring. They began removing the handkerchiefs from their faces, and makeshift stages were erected at almost every street corner where speakers got up to denounce the government. There were the lawyers in their court robes, doctors and nurses in hospital white, bankers, businessmen, laborers, writers, artists, film actors, civil servants from various ministries, housewives again banging pots and pans, now to voice their demands, long processions of trishaw drivers, Buddhist monks in saffron robes, Muslims brandishing green banners, Christian clergymen chanting "Jesus loves democracy"—and even fringe groups such as columns of blind people, and demurely simpering transvestites demanding equal rights.

Communal friction and old grudges were forgotten, and, maybe for the first time ever, all national and political groups across the country joined together for a common cause. In Rangoon, Chins and Kachins showed up at the demonstrations in their traditional tribal costumes and were cheered by onlookers. In Arakan (Rakhine) State in the west, where tension between Buddhists and Muslims had long been prevalent, these two religious groups now marched hand in hand chanting anti-government slogans. The yellow banner of Buddhism fluttered beside Islam's green flag with a crescent moon.

In the Shan State capital of Taunggyi, policemen, doctors, local merchants, government employees, and farmers with bullock carts joined the demonstrations, which attracted nearly one hundred thousand people and resembled a lively country fair. In the Irrawaddy delta towns of Henzada and Bassein, in the oil fields of Chauk and Yenangyaung, in Prome, Magwe, Toungoo, Pyinmana, and Meiktila in the Burmese heartland, altogether millions of people marched against the BSPP government. Strike centers were established in more than 200 of Burma's 314 townships. Rice farmers from the countryside around nearly every town arrived in lorries, bullock carts, and on foot to participate; it was an entire population, rural as well as urban, demanding in unison an end to the military-dominated, one-party rule that had held the country in its suffocating grip for more than two decades.

In street corners all over the capital, popular rock bands and singers played and sang for the demonstrators who marched past chanting slogans. And although everyone was on strike, employees in factories, offices, and other work sites formed their own independent trade unions—something that had been unthinkable for twenty-six years. The unionists of the Burmese Railways declared that they would no longer provide special trains for "dictators of the one-party system." The staff at the meteorology department announced that, henceforth, weather forecasts would be "for the people only and not for the one-party dictatorship."[19]

To demonstrate their unity, most marchers wore red headbands with a dove, symbolizing peace. It was a true "parliament of the streets," in the striking phrase of Cardinal Sin of the Philippines. There was no central leadership for the movement; it was spontaneous in nature and organized by local citizens' committees in the various townships. But soon, student leaders and veteran politicians began to meet at Aung San Suu Kyi's home on University Avenue. It was conveniently located near the university, and the garden was spacious and leafy. And, most important of all, it was the home of the daughter of Burma's national hero, and it developed into an informal "command headquarters" for the pro-democracy movement in Rangoon. But meetings were also held elsewhere. Many older politicians who had been ministers in the pre-1962 era met at U Nu's residence, while former army officers, who had fallen out with the regime, held regular meetings in the home of former defense minister Tin U, now a leading pro-democracy agitator.

For about a month, the creativity of the Burmese psyche flourished again after twenty-six years of silence. Within a week, Rangoon alone had nearly forty independent newspapers and magazines full of political commentaries, biting satires, and witty cartoons ridiculing the ruling elite. These lively, new newspapers—some daily and others intermittent—had fanciful names such as the *Light of Dawn*, the *Liberation Daily*, *Scoop*, the *New Victory*, and the *Newsletter*. Some were handwritten and photocopied or mimeographed, while others were professionally printed, often free of charge because the printing press owners wanted to show that they also supported the pro-democracy movement.

To prove the unanimous support for the pro-democracy movement, one of the new newspapers, the *Phone Maw Journal*—which was named after the first casualty of 1988, a student who had been killed during more limited unrest in March—published in late August a report from the cemetery in Tamwe, a northeastern suburb. After the killings on August 8–12, many corpses had been dumped there without being cremated or the holding of appropriate Buddhist funeral rites. Consequently, the cemetery was believed to be haunted, and after midnight, the newspaper claimed, the ghosts were shouting pro-democracy slogans. Recently, the *Phone Maw Journal* reported, a new unusual chant had been added to the ghosts' repertoire, "Corpses of BSPP members are not allowed to be buried in our cemetery! Stay out! Stay out!"[20]

Even the official newspapers, including the *Guardian* and the *Working People's Daily*, began publishing outspoken political articles. The authorities seemed to tolerate this, but, significantly, the state-run radio and television stations remained unchanged.

What had actually happened? Had the government given up? Opinions were divided. Since the BSPP administration appeared to have collapsed almost everywhere, the army was no longer in evidence, and many government officials had left their homes to take refuge in military camps, some people assumed that this was the case. Others, however, were more cautious. Before long, Burmese sources and diplomats alike reported that actions by agents provocateurs from Burma's secret police, the dreaded Directorate of Defence Services Intelligence (DDSI), became nightly occurrences, including arson, looting, and even an attack on the local UN Food and Agriculture Organization office on September 8.

Army units began hauling rice and other necessities out of the city, and "uniformed men" removed 600 million kyats in Burmese currency from the Union Bank of Burma in Rangoon, which provoked a strong protest from the bank's newly formed, unofficial trade union. By a strange coincidence, there were also nine almost simultaneous prison uprisings in different parts of the country, and nearly nine thousand inmates escaped or were released, without food and money.

Early in the morning of September 6, looters were seen carrying construction material, papers, and office furniture from the compound of a German-sponsored rodent control project in Gyogon-Insein, a Rangoon suburb. At the same time, two army lorries were parked in the yard of the nearby People's Land Settlement Department. The soldiers did not even attempt to stop the looting—instead, they were loading their own lorries with goods from the warehouse. Two hours later, after the soldiers had left with their loot, about two hundred people invaded the offices and the godowns and took almost everything that the soldiers had left behind. Later, in a strongly worded Note Verbale, the German embassy in Rangoon stated, "Army units . . . did actively participate in the looting and did encourage it by their obvious passivity."[21]

Another most remarkable incident had taken place at four o'clock in the morning on August 26, before Suu Kyi was going to give her speech outside the Shwe Dagon. Two pickup trucks carrying between them six people had been stopped for a routine check on 29th Street in central Rangoon by local vigilantes belonging to the citizens' committees. While searching the vehicles, the vigilantes found, to their astonishment, a whole stack of leaflets defaming Suu Kyi and her husband, Michael Aris.

The handwritten leaflets contained crude drawings of the couple and slogans such as, "Call your bastard foreigner and buzz off now!" and "Genocidal prostitute!" Some of the slogans and drawings were startlingly obscene.[22]

The vigilantes immediately apprehended the six and tied them up. A pistol was found in one of the pickup trucks together with ID cards of two of the men. One was Corporal San Lwin and the other Private Soe Naing, both from the DDSI. The six were taken to Thayettaw monastery in central Rangoon, where the monks had set up a court and a temporary prison.

The interrogation was filmed, and the identities of the other DDSI agents were also established. The leader of the team was a DDSI captain, Si Thu, a trusted officer who was close to both Ne Win and his intelligence chief, Khin Nyunt. Pictures of the apprehended DDSI agents were displayed on notice boards all over Rangoon before they were released.[23]

But there were also excesses on the part of the demonstrators, even if these were later grossly exaggerated by the military in its propaganda to justify its claim that it had to step in to "restore law and order." What had started as a carnival-like, Philippine-style "people power" uprising was during the second week of September beginning to turn nasty, and coming more and more to resemble the hunt for the dreaded *tonton macoutes* in Haiti after the fall of "Baby Doc" Duvalier in 1986. Public executions—mostly beheadings—of suspected agents provocateurs sent by the DDSI were becoming an almost daily occurrence in Rangoon.

Aung San Suu Kyi constantly sent her people, both her mature supporters and young students, to try to intervene. In some cases they were successful in saving the lives of suspected agents, but public anger with the military intelligence was so intense that it was almost impossible to stop the lynchings.

During August and September 1988, Suu Kyi's home on University Avenue became a meeting place for the students as well as older pro-democracy activists. Daily meetings were held there, and Suu Kyi lectured her followers about democracy and civil disobedience. But it was not an easy task, and, on September 4, an unusually nasty incident took place at the Kyi Kyi biscuit factory in South Okkalapa, a Rangoon suburb. The local citizens' committee—which had been set up by the pro-democracy movement—got a phone call from someone who claimed a mob was looting the biscuit factory. Nine monks and twelve students were sent to investigate the matter. When they did not come back, several hundred people went down to the factory—only to find that the monks and the students had been captured by the "looters", beaten, and taken away to an enclave for military officers in South Okkalapa.

The crowd gradually swelled to nearly a thousand people, and they demanded the release of their colleagues. Arrows were fired at the crowd, which in turn was armed with daggers and catapults. The godown inside which the "looters" had barricaded themselves was stormed, and the battle lasted all night with nearly one hundred people wounded on both sides. Eventually, sixty-seven of the "looters" were captured. Three of the ones who had been held hostage were freed, while the others were missing, presumed killed.

There was uproar in South Okkalapa for several days afterwards, and Suu Kyi sent some of her people there to calm the people down. But the situation got worse when one of the "looters" confessed that he had been sent by Khin Nyunt's military intelligence to lure monks and students into the factory so that they could be killed. A student who was there later recalled, "About twenty of the captured were beheaded. They seemed drugged and showed no signs of pain during the executions which were carried out by local residents of South Okkalapa. The monks and the students tried to stop the killings and managed to have some of the prisoners ordained as monks. That saved their lives. The people were furious with them."[24]

It was becoming increasingly clear that the military—and especially the DDSI—had not given up, but was plotting a comeback. On September 18, the situation had deteriorated to a point where the military could claim that it had to step in. At four o'clock that afternoon, there was an abrupt break in the state-run radio's afternoon music program. A male voice came on the air, solemnly proclaiming, "In order to bring a timely halt to the deteriorating conditions on all sides all over the country and in the interests of the people, the defence forces have assumed all power in the state with effect from today."[25]

A State Law and Order Restoration Council (SLORC), headed by the chief of staff, Gen. Saw Maung, had been formed to ensure "peace and tranquillity in preparations for democratic multi-party elections." The announcement was followed by strident martial music.

Two hours later, the names of the nineteen members of the SLORC were announced. It included all regional commanders of the Burmese army as well as several other high-ranking military officers from the army, navy, and air force. Its vice chairman was the deputy chief of staff, Lt.-Gen. Than Shwe, and its secretary the director of the DDSI, Khin Nyunt.

An 8 p.m. to 4 a.m. curfew was clamped on Rangoon, and the SLORC with immediate effect banned "gathering, walking, marching in procession, chanting slogans, delivering speeches, agitating, and creating disturbances in the streets by a group of five or more people regardless of whether the act is with the intention of creating disturbances, or of committing a crime, or not."[26] More martial music blared out of the radio.

But it was an unusual "coup." There were none of the characteristics of a military takeover: tanks and troops seizing strategic points in the capital, the arrest of state leaders, a new strongman. The only movements in the streets of Rangoon during the first few hours after the radio announcement were bands of thousands of enraged demonstrators defying the curfew and surging down the streets in the eerie evening twilight. Waving banners, flags and crude, home-made weapons, they shouted angrily at the top of their voices, "*Hwe asuya kya hson base! Hwe asuya kya hson base!*" (Down with the dog government! Down with the dog government!).

The new, self-proclaimed leaders were conspicuous by their absence. Not even the army appeared until late that evening. But when the army trucks, full of troops, and the Bren carriers at last rolled into the city this time, it was an entirely different scene from the August massacre. The organization was impeccable and the operation carried out with icy military efficiency. Any crowd in sight was mowed down systematically, as the army vehicles rumbled down the streets in perfect formation.

After two days of mass killings, the people had been literally shot off the streets. According to the official version no more than "fifteen demonstrators were killed."[27] Diplomatic sources in Rangoon thought otherwise: they reported back to their capitals that at least a thousand people had been killed. Even wounded were carted away in trucks to be disposed of. Melinda Liu wrote in her cover story for *Newsweek* after the massacre, "Witnesses at the cemetery said they heard cries of shooting victims who had been brought to Kyandaw [crematorium] while they were still alive—and were cremated along with the corpses."

At Rangoon General Hospital she saw

> victims with mangled limbs, chest wounds and legs in blood-stained casts. In the emergency ward, gunshot victims writhed on rusting gurneys, dripping blood onto the grimy floor. Undersupplied at the best of times, the hospital was running desperately low on blood and plasma. It was also running short of morgue space. I saw thirty bodies piled helter-skelter in the refrigerated vault. . . . One man was missing the top of his head; a ten-year-old boy had a bullet hole in the middle of his forehead."[28]

The senseless massacre was condemned immediately by all Western democracies, and by Japan and India. A Western ambassador in Rangoon lashed out at the new junta, "It's so shameful what's happening. I have no words for it. It's just a small group of people who want to consolidate their power and are willing to shoot down school children and unarmed demonstrators to do so." Rangoon, he said, was "like a city occupied by a foreign army."[29] Foreign aid was cut off by the United States, Australia, Britain, Germany, and Japan.

The new junta, for its part, ordered the people to return to work. On October 2, the SLORC warned over the state-run radio that "anyone who prevents, obstructs, or interferes with workers returning to work . . . will be dealt with sternly."[30] On the following day, the six-week-long general strike collapsed. Facing threats of dismissal and short of cash, civil servants and laborers sullenly trickled back to their offices and factories.

But the military intervention on September 18 also triggered a mass exodus to Burma's border areas, where the country's ethnic insurgents were active. Following the second massacre in September, many of the urban activists no longer believed in peaceful demonstrations. They wanted to take up arms against the new junta in Rangoon.

Thousands of students boarded cars and buses bound for Moulmein and Kawkareik, and from there trekked through the jungles and over the hills to the Thai border near Mae Sot, or to the rugged Three Pagodas Pass northwest of Kanchanaburi. From Mandalay and Sagaing, students fled north to the Kachin Hills and eventually reached the Kachin rebel headquarters at Pa Jau, close to the Chinese frontier. Others headed west, towards India, and crossed into Mizoram and Manipur. Many activists from Arakan State filtered into northeastern Bangladesh. During the last weeks of September, approximately eight thousand to ten thousand, mostly young people, left the cities, towns, and villages of central Burma for the border.

On November 5, a meeting was held at Wangkha, a Karen rebel base close to the Thai frontier. After lengthy deliberations, the participants decided to set up an umbrella organization of students who had fled to the Thai, Chinese, and Bangladeshi borders. It was called the All-Burma Students Democratic Front (ABSDF), and Htun Aung Gyaw, a student activist in his mid-thirties, was elected chairman. An alliance was formed between the ethnic rebels who had been fighting the Rangoon regime for decades, and the more militant wing of the pro-democracy movement.

Among the activists who stayed behind in Rangoon, an entirely different movement took shape. The one-party system—as well as the Burmese Way to Socialism—had been abolished, and people were actually free to register new political parties, as well as private companies. At least the uprising had forced the authorities to introduce what seemed to be some fundamental changes. Even if the thousands of students who had fled to the border areas did not believe that fighting for democracy in the urban areas was possible, many NLD activists and others began to take advantage of the new rules. Preparations began for the formation of political parties, while political meetings were held on a daily basis in Rangoon, not in public, but in private homes. The uprising had, after all, ignited unprecedented political activities among the Burmese population. There was no freedom, but the desire for freedom was unstoppable.

On September 24, the old BSPP—which had been officially dissolved in the wake of the pro-democracy uprising—was reborn as the National Unity Party, NUP. The name change fooled nobody; the NUP inherited the buildings and machinery of the BSPP, and the entire central committee of the "new" party consisted of second-rung ex-BSPP leaders with close army connections. Its chairman, Tha Kyaw, was a former BSPP minister. Thura Kyaw Zwa, the so-called butcher of Sagaing, was appointed local NUP leader in Pegu.

The same day, the pro-democracy forces met in Rangoon, and on the twenty-seventh, the National League for Democracy (NLD), was formed. Aung Gyi, Tin U, and Aung San Suu Kyi were elected to the top positions in the new party—as chairman, vice chairman, and general secretary respectively. Although she was officially number three in the hierarchy, Suu Kyi was the focal point of the pro-democracy movement. When she had first appeared in public outside the Shwe Dagon on August 26, most people had probably showed up out of curiosity; she was Aung San's daughter and that was why everybody knew her. Over subsequent months—and especially after the formation of the SLORC—she matured politically and developed an identity of her own. She gave speeches all over the country, wrote letters to the United Nations Commission on Human Rights, and met foreign diplomats in Rangoon. In a talk at the Asia Society in New York on November 29, Burton Levin, the then US ambassador to Burma, commented:

> Even though she is married to a foreigner, nonetheless she touches a chord among the whole spectrum of Burmese life. The first time she came to my house for lunch, I had every one of my servants just lining up. It was like, in American terms, one of these nutty rock stars appearing at a high school. It was really something. She's got charisma, she's bright, she knows how to speak, she's come to the fore.[31]

Having established the NLD, Suu and her colleagues also announced—after some hesitation—that they would be willing to participate in the general election that the SLORC, after all, had promised. But it was clear that the young organization was inexperienced and not sure how to deal with this extraordinary situation.

Furthermore, the NLD was not, and never became, a properly organized political party. Rather, it was the outcome of a spontaneous mass movement for democracy, which had actually begun in March that year, when the first clashes between students and security forces had taken place. Then, in June, there had been more demonstrations, and killings of young protesters. Word of an imminent popular uprising had spread across the country, and although the mass movement that had emerged on 8.8.88 had been well-organized, it had no central leadership or common strategy.

When the NLD was set up, local committees were formed equally spontaneously all over the country. People could no longer demonstrate, but it was possible to hold meetings and discussions under the aegis of the NLD banner. There were local NLD organizations in remote towns and villages, the existence of which were unknown to the party headquarters in Rangoon.[32]

The party's program, which was adopted at the founding meeting, resembled a manifesto more than a plan for action. It consisted of eight pages and emphasized close relations with the United Nations and the international community, the importance of free enterprise and an export-oriented economy, and free internal trade in rice. Its policy on the ethnic minorities stated that "the Union of Burma was founded upon the unity and common aspirations of all the peoples of the nation. The forty-year history of their relations has been a chapter of misfortune verging on the tragic. . . . We must seek a lasting solution to the problems of the ethnic minorities."[33]

The program also noted that there were "no less than thirteen groups of insurgents" along Burma's borders, "a situation which is sapping the strength and resources of the nation. The development of the country has suffered greatly since approximately 40 percent of the national budget has to be devoted to defense requirements." The NLD's assessment of the situation in Burma was grim, but also limited to general statements such as these. Despite the relative vagueness of the program, however, the NLD attracted a mass following of lawyers, doctors, other professionals, writers, journalists, and students. There were perhaps fewer members in the countryside, but there was no doubt as to whom the rural population supported as well. Soon after the formation of the NLD, Suu Kyi embarked on a strenuous program. She made her first trip upcountry in October 1988 to meet people in preparations for the promised general elections. Over a period of thirteen days she visited more than fifty towns and villages in Pegu, Magwe, Sagaing, and Mandalay Divisions, as well as Shan State. Tens of thousands of people turned out to see her, in effect defying the notorious SLORC decree banning gatherings of five or more people.

The army surprisingly did not interfere; there were even reports of soldiers presenting flowers to the entourage, underlining the fact that her father's name, and by heritage also hers, was magic among virtually every sector of Burmese society. At the same time, there were serious internal problems in the NLD. On December 3, its chairman, Aung Gyi, resigned and quit the party because it refused to expel eight alleged communists, or former communists, from the organization. They were all middle-aged, and they certainly had been involved in leftist politics in the past, but now asserted that they had become "true democrats." Aung Gyi did not believe them, and on December 16, he set up his own political party, the Union Nationals Democracy Party (UNDP). The

NLD was not a cohesive organization, and it consisted of several interest groups with various backgrounds. However, Aung Gyi clearly overstated the importance of the former communists, and, hardly surprisingly, his UNDP soon faded away and never left a mark on the political scene in Burma.

Unperturbed, Suu Kyi continued campaigning for her cause. Also in December, she went to the Moulmein area in southeastern Burma. But this time, army vehicles mounted with loudspeakers cruised the streets and told the public not to come out and greet her. Thousands defied that order, and the welcome she received in Moulmein was as enthusiastic as the one in the north. After the trip, thirteen NLD workers were arrested, and on December 19, the SLORC issued a stern warning to the people "to behave. . . . It is necessary to abide by rules, orders, laws, and regulations."[34] Evidently, the SLORC was beginning to realize that a political leader had emerged whom it would not be easy to control or cow into submission.

The next big challenge to the SLORC—and to Ne Win, who was still pulling strings from behind the scenes—came at the turn of the tumultuous year of 1988. On December 27, Suu Kyi's bedridden mother, Khin Kyi, died. Huge crowds began to gather outside Suu Kyi's home, and the military authorities issued a stern warning against "disturbances" during the funeral.

The new year 1989 was ushered in, and many people began asking what it would bring to crisis-ridden Burma. On January 1, SLORC chairman Gen. Saw Maung, DDSI chief Brig.-Gen. Khin Nyunt, and the home and religious affairs minister, Maj.-Gen. Phone Myint, called at University Avenue to sign the condolence book.

Although Suu Kyi had had earlier meetings with Phone Myint, this was the first time she had met Saw Maung and Khin Nyunt. She invited them for tea, and their discussions were described by eyewitnesses as "very lively," indicating that she seized the opportunity to remind the military of earlier promises of "free and fair elections" and a return to democracy.

The following day the funeral took place. More than a hundred thousand people—some sources said up to a million—marched through the streets of Rangoon, from the house on University Avenue to a special tomb that had been built near U Thant's burial place close to the Shwe Dagon Pagoda. The marchers carried NLD flags and banners, and party workers ensured discipline and took care of security; the troops that had been ordered out to oversee the event nervously clutched their rifles in the background, probably feeling their isolation as there was actually no need for their presence.

Groups of students sang anti-government songs and chanted in unison, "We won't forget our comrades who fell in the struggle for democracy!" and "We won't kneel to oppression!" The march, which was the first since SLORC took over on September 18, passed peacefully. Min Ko Naing, a charismatic and elusive student leader who had been at the frontlines during the uprising and then gone into hiding, appeared briefly and told the marchers to behave with discipline and dignity.

Surprisingly, Suu Kyi's brother Aung San U, who had become a US citizen, had been granted a visa to attend the funeral and paid his first visit to Rangoon in many years. But his presence caused less of a stir than expected; he was seen in the funeral procession, called on Aung Gyi, and then returned to California.

Several foreign envoys also participated in the march. Significantly, the ambassadors of Japan, the United States, Britain, Italy, France, and West Germany flew out that afternoon to Bangkok to avoid attending another function on January 4—Burma's Independence Day celebrations, organized by the military. The ambassador of India had left a few days earlier for the same reason. Western countries and Japan had cut their foreign aid programs following the massacres in Rangoon. The US Senate had been the first to condemn the carnage, and on September 28, the British foreign secretary, Sir Geoffrey Howe, in an outspoken address in the UN's General Assembly, had lashed out against the SLORC: "In Burma we have been appalled at the killing of unarmed demonstrators, women and children, which has taken place. . . . The Burmese authorities must recognise that the only way to a lasting solution to the country's internal crisis lies in meeting the desire of the Burmese people for greater freedom and multi-party democracy."[35]

It is still an open question to what extent Khin Kyi had influenced Suu

Kyi to enter politics. But Tin Moe, a well-known Burmese poet who was close to the family, believes Suu Kyi consulted her mother and obtained her approval before becoming a public figure in August 1988.[36] Khin Kyi was, after all, the link between Suu Kyi and a father she could not remember. Whatever Suu Kyi knew about her father had been passed on by her mother, and Khin Kyi's dislike of Ne Win, Aung San's rival and foe, was no secret. According to Tin Moe, Suu Kyi must have learned a "great deal about Burma's politics from her mother." The poet was often invited in the early 1980s to visit Khin Kyi at her lakeside home in Rangoon. Suu Kyi would be there, visiting from her home in England, and Khin Kyi "would chat with them while gardening or sitting in the kitchen." And she always talked about politics. "In front of her mother, Daw Suu looked like an innocent child, not knowing anything, including politics and things like that," said Tin Moe.[37]

In many ways, Khin Kyi's funeral marked a watershed in immediate post-coup politics. The pro-democracy movement had demonstrated its strength as well as its ability to control the crowds, the Western democracies had expressed in no uncertain terms where their sympathies lay, and the SLORC found itself isolated and estranged from both its own people and the international, democratic community.

From then on, the confrontation between the SLORC and the NLD escalated. The harassment that had begun during Suu Kyi's campaign tour of the Moulmein area intensified during two subsequent trips to the Irrawaddy delta region, and to Tavoy and Mergui in Tenasserim Division in January and February. In several towns in the delta, people were told to stay indoors, and barbed-wire fences were erected across major streets leading to the places where she was going to deliver her speeches. Thirty-four NLD workers were arrested in the wake of her tour.

Anti-SLORC demonstrations began again in several cities and towns across the country in March, when students and pro-democracy parties marked the death of student martyr Maung Phone Maw. Troops and armed police patrolled the streets of Rangoon, and many more student activists were arrested, among them Min Ko Naing, who was found and apprehended in a safe house in the capital. The situation became even more confrontational when Ne Win himself reappeared at a dinner party in Rangoon on March 27, Armed Forces Day, effectively laying to rest all speculation that he was out of the picture despite his formal resignation the year before.

In a much publicized incident in the Irrawaddy delta town of Danubyu on April 5, Myint Oo, an army captain, ordered his soldiers to load their guns and aim at Suu Kyi, who was walking down a street in the town with her entourage. She told her followers to take to the sides of the road while she calmly walked down the center towards the soldiers. "It seemed so much simpler to provide them with a single target than to bring everyone else in," she later said. Before the troops could open fire, however, a major intervened. But the fact that Myint Oo shortly afterwards was promoted to major indicated that he had official approval for his action.[38]

The reappearance of the old dictator Ne Win was ridiculed in a traditional Burmese way by the pro-democracy movement, which staged a slogan competition outside the NLD's headquarters in Rangoon during *thingyan*, the water festival that marks the Buddhist New Year in mid-April. Infuriated by this, the SLORC detained several students who had taken part in the event, and, at about the same time, arrests began of NLD grassroots organizers in a number of upcountry towns: Pakokku, Taunggyi, Kyauk-padaung, Monywa, and Myinmu.

On June 18, the SLORC went a step further in its attempt to suppress the reborn democracy movement. A new draconian printing law was promulgated, aimed at preventing the critics of the regime from issuing "unauthorized publications." In effect, it ensured the monopoly of the *Working People's Daily*—yet again the only official newspaper in the country and now back under government control—on information.[39]

Responding to these moves, Suu Kyi became increasingly outspoken in her criticism of the military regime. She also, for the first time, openly attacked Ne Win, accusing him of being responsible for Burma's economic and political misery. She implied that nothing would fundamentally change as long as the old strongman was still there, pretending that he had retired.

"The Movement of 1989," as it became known, was in many ways more significant than the upheaval of 1988. The spectacle of massive, restive crowds dancing down the streets, shouting slogans, and waving banners, now belonged to the past. Instead, tens of thousands stood in silence, listening attentively for hours at end to an entirely new message: democracy through discipline, responsibility, and nonviolent struggle. The speaker was Suu Kyi, whose stamina and courage infused hope and self-confidence among her massive audiences across the country.

Since her first appearance outside the Shwe Dagon in August 1988 she had delivered more than a thousand speeches across the country. Not surprisingly, her speeches had echoed her interpretations of themes from her father's writings that had emerged during her research in Britain, Japan, and India: the dependence of freedom on discipline, fair treatment of political opponents, and a deep distaste for power-mongering and behind-the-scenes maneuverings. More informal talks had focused on the importance of reading books and on people taking responsibility for their own neighborhoods, where grassroots democracy should begin. Aung San's legacy also appeared in statements addressing the unresolved problems of continued militarism in Burma, as well as the political factionalism that her father had foreseen, and which had overtaken him at his assassination.

It was obvious that this new movement posed a much more serious challenge to the regime than the street demonstrations in 1988. A new power center was emerging, threatening the old order. Among all the politicians, old and new, who had emerged or reemerged on the Burmese scene since 1988, Suu Kyi stood out as the only one who could unify all segments of Burmese society: the urban as well as the rural population, Burma's many ethnic minorities, young student radicals, and older, more moderate pro-democracy campaigners. Perhaps even more importantly, soldiers who were sent out to disperse the crowds began to get down from their army lorries to listen to her message. As the daughter of the founder of the Burmese army, she was in a position to rally even the armed forces behind her. The old rulers were becoming redundant, and they would soon belong to history if this young woman was allowed to continue her countrywide campaign for a new Burma.

From the SLORC's point of view, an extremely dangerous situation was emerging. Under Suu Kyi's leadership, the NLD had developed into a clear alternative to the established order, and a new pro-democracy movement was taking shape that was more experienced and better organized than the spontaneous uprising of 1988.

The situation became even tenser in the weeks before the forty-second anniversary of Aung San's assassination on July 19, 1989. Suu Kyi had declared that she would march—in a peaceful and disciplined manner—with thousands of her followers to pay respects to her fallen father, and not take part in the SLORC-organized ceremony.

However, on July 18, army trucks equipped with loudspeakers crisscrossed Rangoon to announce the SLORC's latest decree under which anyone opposing it could be tried by military tribunal. Those found guilty would receive one of three sentences: three years' imprisonment with hard labor, life imprisonment, or execution. Early in the morning of the nineteenth, an estimated ten thousand soldiers, including artillery and armored car units, moved into Rangoon to reinforce the troops already stationed there. Roadblocks were erected at strategic points in the city, all major hospitals in the capital were told to expect casualties, and the telephone and telex lines between Burma and the outside world were cut. In order to avoid another bloodbath, Suu Kyi called off her planned march.

On July 20, soldiers entered Suu Kyi's compound on University Avenue. Her young followers, who had gathered there every day since August the year before, were either arrested or sent home. Suu Kyi was placed under house arrest "for up to one year"—hardly by coincidence well beyond the promised general election, which now had been scheduled for May 1990. NLD chairman Tin U was also placed under house arrest, while in sweeps all over the country thousands of party activists were arrested and offices closed down by the military authorities.

The mighty NLD had been decapitated, and its second-echelon leaders, mostly retired army officers who had joined the pro-democracy movement in 1988, took over. Open mass opposition to the SLORC regime came to an end. For the first time, not only younger activists but also the leaders of the pro-democracy movement—who had organized previous protests—were targeted and arrested. The NLD had emerged and grown as a movement. And despite the weakness of the second-rung leaders who took over in July 1989, the desire for progress and freedom was not dead.

CHAPTER 3

THE DEIFICATION OF AUNG SAN SUU KYI

No one came more to epitomize the Burmese people's desire for a better future than Aung San Suu Kyi. Even in complete isolation under house arrest in her home on University Avenue, where she remained for six years, she was still a powerful pro-democracy icon. No one saw her, no one heard her speak. But the images of 1988 were still fresh in people's memory. Even the outside world was captivated by the charismatic, young woman who had dared the guns of Burma's military dictatorship, showing no fear and rallying people behind her wherever she appeared.

The incident in the small Irrawaddy delta town of Danubyu in April 1989—when she walked towards the guns that were aimed at her—even made it to Hollywood. It was a central scene in John Boorman's 1995 film *Beyond Rangoon*, which was set in Burma but filmed largely in Malaysia. With Adelle Lutz playing the part of Suu Kyi, it centers on a fictitious young American doctor, Laura Bowman, who happened to be in Burma in August 1988 and then was caught up in the whirlwind of events. She witnessed the massacres and eventually managed to escape to Thailand with a group of Burmese students. The tagline of the film is "Truth has a witness."[1]

Even so, the actors in the movie seemed to have little knowledge of what was actually happening in Burma. When asked what her response was to being asked to play Suu Kyi, Lutz replied, "I got really giddy. She's alive and under house arrest, and she was elected president with over

85 per cent of the vote."[2] Whatever the misconceptions, Suu Kyi versus the SLORC became in most people's minds the Beauty and the Beast—a courageous woman against one of the world's most brutal dictatorships. The battle lines could not be clearer, the divisions more precise. But the situation in Burma since the massive uprising for democracy in 1988 has never been that simple.

Little is known about how Suu Kyi spent her first period under house arrest, from July 20, 1989 to July 10, 1995. But, according to one of her biographers, Whitney Stewart, she set up a daily routine to keep her mind and body strong and "only varied that routine on Saturday and Sunday, when she let herself enjoy leisurely activity."[3] She would get up at 4:30 a.m. to mediate, "concentrating on her breathing and being aware of everything around her." Suu Kyi herself later told a reporter, "House arrest has given me the opportunity to try to overcome my own weaknesses and faults, especially through meditation. . . . I am very short-tempered, but I think I am far less short-tempered now than I used to be."[4] She also "read a lot of biographies. They taught me how other people faced problems in life. Mandela. Sakharov. Mother Teresa."

After meditating for an hour, she listened to the radio, did some exercise, read voraciously, and had lunch prepared by her faithful maid, a Karen named Maria. She would then read and write some more, and wrap up the day with a bath and listening to the radio again before going to sleep.[5]

According to Stewart, "There were times in her detention when Suu Kyi had no money for food. Her usual weight of 106 pounds [53 kilograms] dropped to below 100, and her hair fell out." To get money, she arranged through Maria and the military intelligence officer who was attached to liaise with her to sell some of the items in the house, including furniture, a bathtub, and an air conditioner—though not her piano, as it was believed at the time. Neighbors had not heard her play the piano for quite some time, which sparked the rumors. It later became known that she just didn't want to play it because it was out of tune.

Suu Kyi received some money for the furniture, but the SLORC did not sell it but stored it. When the military offered to give the furniture back to her as a gift, she flatly refused. She insisted on buying certain items back.[6]

Michael and the boys had left Burma shortly after she was placed under house arrest, but he was allowed to send her books and other reading material through the diplomatic pouch. Meanwhile, Michael began lobbying internationally for Suu Kyi's cause with considerable success, but discreetly and always in the background.

Meanwhile, the lady behind the solid iron gates of 54 University Avenue received one international honor after another. In 1990, she was made an honorary fellow at St. Hugh's College in Oxford, where she had studied in the 1960s. In October of that year, she was awarded, in absentia, the Rafto Human Rights Prize, which was set up in honor of Thorolf Rafto, a Norwegian proponent of improving human rights behind the Iron Curtain.

The Rafto prize ceremony is held in the Norwegian city of Bergen, and Suu Kyi's recognition there led to the 1991 Nobel Peace Prize. Norway became her most faithful and dedicated supporter in the international arena. She also became an honorary member of International PEN and the University of London's Student Union. She received an honorary doctorate in political science from Thammasat University in Thailand and an honorary doctorate of laws from Queen's University, Canada. The Danish labor movement honored her as well, and in 1992, UNESCO awarded her the International Simon Bolivar Prize. The following year, the Center for Human Rights and Constitutional Law in Los Angeles named her the recipient of its Victor Jara International Human Rights Award, and, in December 1994, the Forum of Democratic Leaders in the Asia-Pacific made her an honorary adviser to its board—and all this while she was still under house arrest.

Her contacts with the outside world were restricted to a few family visits, and she heard about the NLD's May 1990 election victory—and the 1991 Nobel Peace Prize—on the radio. It must have strengthened her resolve, but also reinforced her main weakness. Kyi Maung, the former army colonel who took over the leadership of the NLD when Suu Kyi and Tin U were placed under house arrest, once told Alan Clements, an

American writer who has been a Buddhist monk in Burma, "Suu has got a devotion bordering on fanaticism, to the point of fault, I think. She is a real workaholic." But he also said that she would readily admit it, and "Suu is like a daughter to me."[7]

Kyi Maung was very close to Suu Kyi's family. Having joined the student union under Aung San, he later served with the nationalist forces during World War II, and studied at the Imperial Military Academy in Japan from 1943 to 1945. A serving army colonel, he had been one of the original members of Ne Win's Revolutionary Council in 1962, but had resigned in 1963. Like many other army officers of his generation, he had joined the NLD in 1988.

Suu Kyi's stubbornness—as well as her personal dilemma—was evident in her relationship with Michael Aris. On the one hand, he was lobbying successfully for her in the outside world but, on the other, he was a citizen of the former colonial power, and the military government never failed to mention that in its propaganda tirades against her. She was called "Mrs. Michael Aris" in the official newssheet, the *Working People's Daily*.

In 1997, the government's propaganda department published as a book a collection of articles by someone calling himself Hpe Kan Kaung, "one of the regime's infamous journalists," according to Dutch Burma scholar Gustaaf Houtman.[8] The book reflects the image of Suu Kyi that the regime wants to project:

> This person whom the Puppet Princess thinks is very good to her as a spouse is no ordinary person. He is a good acquaintance of people of high society and aristocracy of England and moves in and out of the Oxford circle of scholars and keeps company of famous reporters and is capable of influencing them to write whatever he would like them to. He is a great director and puppeteer who can pull the strings.[9]

The very thought of the quiet and reserved academic Michael Aris being a "director" and a "puppeteer" is, of course, absurd, and it is hard to believe that many Burmese took Hpe Kan Kaung and his crude rantings seriously.

On the other hand, apart from a brief reference to her foreign husband at the mass rally outside the Shwe Dagon on August 26, 1988, Suu Kyi has seldom mentioned her family. Whether she liked it or not, she had to put her country and its politics ahead of her own husband and sons, and when she decided to enter politics in 1988, her marriage to a foreigner did become an issue.

In her own words, when Michael and the boys came to see her on a few rare occasions, she was filled with "mixed emotions. . . . I know that whatever sacrifices my family and I have to make are very small compared to the troubles and uncertainties suffered by those of my colleagues who have not the protection of a famous father."[10]

Not surprisingly, the sons suffered as a result. Alexander, the older of the two, began studying at Georgetown University's School of Foreign Service in 1990, but left two years later without finishing his course. He had serious trouble coping with his mother's incarceration. Kim, the younger son, used to play in a rock group with friends in Oxford, and is more easygoing. But he has also suffered psychologically both from growing up without a mother, and from being the son of the world's most famous political prisoner. He was only eleven during the upheavals of 1988, and twelve when he was separated from his mother.

Barbara Bradley, an American journalist, found that "there's something of a clinical quality to Suu Kyi's resolve."[11] She gives as an example a request by Suu Kyi in the spring of 1992 to meet with two political advisers from the NLD who were incarcerated in Rangoon's Insein Prison. The request was denied, but the authorities said they would allow a visit by Michael, who she then had not seen for over two years. She reportedly replied, "No, you cannot do that. If you have such a thing in mind, you must ask me first. Without my permission, I will not receive anybody."[12]

On May 5, her husband arrived anyway, and, as Bradley suggests, was most likely unaware of the feud. "She stood on the steps and said, 'you cannot come here,'" according to what Kyi Maung later told Bradley. He had to sleep in her aunt's house beside the main building in the compound. On another occasion, she staged a hunger strike and refused to eat because she would not accept goods from the government. She was perhaps inspired by Gandhi, but he went on hunger strikes in the full view of the masses of people around him for maximum impact on the public at large and the international community. Many would argue that going on a hunger strike while under detention has little propaganda value and only inflicts suffering on the person refusing to eat. In the end, a compromise was reached, and that was when she began selling her furniture to get money to buy food.

After her book *Freedom from Fear and Other Writings*—a collection of essays edited by Michael Aris—was published by Penguin in 1991, her financial problems were solved. Her maid Maria was able to withdraw money from the Rangoon bank account into which the royalties had been paid. However, the money from the Nobel Peace Prize which she received in December that year—$1.3 million—was used to establish a health and education trust in support of the Burmese people, and did not go to her personally.

Freedom from Fear is in many ways a remarkable book. The title actually comes from an essay that she wrote in 1991. It was smuggled out of Burma by Michael Aris, and appeared in various versions in the *Far Eastern Economic Review*, *Times Literary Supplement*, *New York Times*, *Times of India*, and in various newspapers in Germany, Norway, and Iceland. It was in that article that she authored the famous phrase, "It is not power that corrupts but fear. Fear of losing power corrupts those who wield it and fear of the scourge of power corrupts those who are subject to it."[13] The book carried a foreword by Vaclav Havel, then president of undivided Czechoslovakia.

Freedom from Fear soon became a bestseller, mainly because of Suu Kyi's own popularity at home and internationally. Apart from essays such as the one that gave the book its title, it also contained her previously published biography of her father, her study of intellectual life in Burma and India under colonialism, and various speeches she had made during the upheavals of 1988 and 1989, including her controversial speech in Kachin State on April 27, 1989, in which she belittled the importance of ethnic identity. But, at that time, little or no attention was paid to her political weaknesses. She was already becoming a saint who was above criticism.

During 1989–95, very few were allowed to see her apart from her husband and their sons. One of the few exceptions was when US congressman Bill Richardson came on an unexpected visit on February 14, 1994. Accompanied by the resident representative of the United Nations Development Programme, Jehan Raheem, and *New York Times* reporter Philip Shenon, they met in Suu Kyi's home. Earlier that day, they had met SLORC secretary Khin Nyunt, who, despite his active involvement in suppressing the pro-democracy movement in 1988, was beginning to show some flexibility. Richardson, a Democrat, was close to then US president Bill Clinton, an ardent admirer of Suu Kyi and leader of the country that was the staunchest critic of the SLORC. By arranging this visit, the SLORC was to "send a positive humanitarian gesture to the US president," and get unofficial access to Clinton to ward off further sanctions and other punitive actions by Washington.[14] Clinton had also studied at Oxford in the 1960s, but it is not clear whether he and Suu Kyi ever met there, as many Burmese believe.

Both Richardson and Suu Kyi were critical of a National Convention that the SLORC had set up after refusing to honor the outcome of the 1990 election. The elected parliament was never convened. Instead, in 1992, an assembly called the "National Convention"—consisting of 700 delegates of whom only 100 came from the ranks of the 485 elected MPS—was set up. The rest were handpicked by the military. The task of this assembly was to draft a new constitution, as Khin Nyunt had laid out in July 1990.

For the first time since she was placed under house arrest, Suu Kyi was able to outline her views on what was happening in Burma at that time. She said she thought

> of the people every day, including my colleagues in the NLD. But the people must be united if they want to get democracy. When I first started the NLD, some students went off to the border. Some old and respectable people, not the students, suggested taking up arms. Many people felt arms were the only way to oppose the military. There were so many views. But the essential thing was to stay united. Even now I will not disavow the students. We others must not be quick to condemn the methods of others.[15]

Despite her commitment to nonviolence and civil disobedience, Suu Kyi refused to distance herself from the armed struggle of the students, which may seem like a contradiction. It should also be remembered that she came from a military family background; her famous father was, after all, the founder of the Burmese army.

She also gave her views on economic and other sanctions, which Western countries and, to a lesser extent, Japan, had imposed on Burma after the 1988 massacres. "Is existing trade with Burma really helping the people or allowing the government to dig in its heels?" Reading between the lines, it was obvious what she thought of foreign entities trading with Burma. Richardson quoted US Burma expert David Steinberg as suggesting that the approach used by Japan and Singapore—greater engagement with the SLORC—would be a better way to enhance democratic progress in Burma than the hard-line policies of the West. Suu Kyi shot back with a rhetorical, "How do they believe this will improve the situation?"

She then went on to outline her views on the future:

> I have a vision of a country where we can sort out our problems by talking to each other. Democracy won't solve all our problems. I've always said this. Establishing democracy here is only the beginning. It is not a perfect system but it's better than all the others. . . . We can have democracy the Asian way, the Burmese way. Whatever system develops here will become unique to this country. Democracy is not the same as in the US and UK. There will always be differences. But some fundamental principles are abiding. Having imposed the "Burmese Way to Socialism" on us for so many years, I now dread the SLORC wanting to impose its idea of a "Burmese Way to Democracy."

It is not clear from the transcript of the conversation exactly what kind of democracy that would be. In fact, Suu Kyi has been vague on the entire subject of democracy, and she has never spelled it out in more concrete terms than a wish for a dialogue with Burma's rulers, and some kind of national reconciliation. During her talk with Richardson, she refuted, in her own inimitable way, the claim by some of her critics that she had been unwilling to talk to the SLORC. "I only refused to see some of them because they have not behaved like officers and gentlemen," she said.

Richardson found a determined and principled woman who just refused to be intimidated. But her strong religious, almost mystical, streak was also beginning to show. She told the visitors that

> a ninety-year-old abbot I knew gave me two pieces of advice. He told me that, in order to achieve happiness, you must be prepared to suffer. He also warned me that anyone who indulges in honest politics must be prepared to be reviled. Monks like him have given me some wonderful advice over the years. Though on old and religious man, he certainly understood politics in Burma.

Richardson then told Suu Kyi that he believed that the key to democratic change in Burma was dialogue between her and Khin Nyunt. Suu Kyi replied, "Between the SLORC and the NLD, and between the NLD and the democratic forces. I don't want to see a personality cult develop. When we set up a democracy here, we need to base it on solid principles, not individual persons." But a personality cult had already taken firm root, at home in Burma as well as abroad.

There is nothing unusual in Burmese history about charismatic personalities emerging when the country is in crisis. But that a woman had to take on this momentous task in a basically patriarchal society such as Burma's at first surprised many outside observers. Still, as US Burma scholar Josef Silverstein has pointed out, in Burmese history there are also instances when women have attained positions of power and influence.[16] Silverstein mentions Shain Saw Bu, a fifteenth-century heroine who ruled the country and, upon retirement, devoted herself to religion. Supayalat, the queen of the last king of Burma, Thibaw, was more powerful than her husband. Daw Mya Sein, a distinguished scholar, author, and secretary of the Burmese Women's Association, was chosen to represent the women of Burma at a special Burma Round Table Conference in London in 1931. According to the minutes from the proceedings in London:

> The women of Burma occupy a position of freedom and independence not attained in other provinces (of British India). Socially there is practical equality between the sexes. Purdah is unknown; women take their full share with men in the economic life of the country and the percentage of literates among women is far higher than elsewhere.[17]

Following independence in 1948 and the establishment of a federal system, the prime minister had the right to select representatives of the ethnic states in his cabinet. In 1953, U Nu appointed Ba Maung Chein to represent Karen State. She later broke with U Nu, but, until then, she was the first woman in Burma to hold a cabinet post.

Few women, however, achieved leadership in their own right and, perhaps not surprisingly in an army-dominated administration, women came to play a much smaller role during the military dictatorship that began in 1962.

The NLD was an entirely different entity, and when it was set up in September 1988, several women came to occupy important posts. Daw Myint Myint Khin, a prominent Rangoon lawyer, was elected to the top leadership, and Ma Thanegi, a writer and expert in Burmese puppet theater, became Suu Kyi's personal assistant.[18] Both Myint Myint Khin and Ma Thanegi were among the many NLD workers who were arrested and sent to Insein Prison when Suu Kyi was placed under house arrest in July 1989.

But Suu Kyi is unique even in a Burmese context. She is the only Burmese woman to have won worldwide fame. And she is a leader in her own right. In Burma, there is no other person who can even remotely match her charisma and her ability to mobilize the people. But that is also a weakness of Burma's pro-democracy movement. It is almost entirely dependent on her personality and guidance, even today.

Her international stature was further enhanced when, on October 14, 1991, the Nobel Peace prize committee in Oslo, Norway, announced that she was that year's recipient of the world's most prestigious peace award. Congratulatory messages and statements came from all over the world, and in the seedy neighborhoods of lower Phrakhanong and Suan

Phlu in Bangkok—where thousands of illegal migrants from Burma hid from the Thai police—parties were held all night. On a day like that, the Thai immigration authorities would not dare to bother anyone from Burma, and the illegals could, for once, feel proud of who they were and the country they came from. In Singapore, Burmese seamen on shore leave were dancing in the streets, completely indifferent to what the rigid authorities of the city-state—a close ally of the junta in Rangoon—thought about them.

On December 10, Suu Kyi's elder son, Alexander, received the prize on her behalf at a grand ceremony in Oslo City Hall. Everyone was moved by the speech that he delivered before an audience of several hundred dignitaries, including the king and queen of Norway. Alexander, who was only eighteen at the time, spoke calmly and firmly, although he touched on painful and sensitive issues:

> I stand before you here today to accept on behalf of my mother, Aung San Suu Kyi, the greatest of all prizes, the Nobel Peace Prize. Because circumstances do not permit my mother to be here in person, I will do my best to convey the sentiments I believe she would wish to express. Firstly, I know that she would begin by saying that she accepts the Nobel Peace Prize not in her own name but in the name of all the people of Burma, . . . and no one must underestimate their plight. The plight of those in the countryside and towns, living in poverty and destitution, those in prison, battered and tortured; the plight of young people, the hope of Burma, dying of malaria in the jungles to which they have fled; that of the Buddhist monks, beaten and dishonoured. . . . It is on their behalf that I thank you, from my heart, for this supreme honour.[19]

Alexander's mentioning of the students who had fled to the jungle was daring, considering that they were being sheltered by armed rebel groups, and Suu Kyi and the NLD were supposed to be legal political entities, even though constantly harassed by the country's military authorities. But he then went on to refer to other sides of his mother's personality, qualities and views that many would find somewhat obscure:

> Although my mother is often described as a political dissident who strives by peaceful means for democratic change, we should remember that her quest is basically spiritual. As she has said, "The quintessential revolution is that of the spirit," and she has written of the "essential spiritual aims" of the struggle. The realization of this depends solely on human responsibility. At the root of that responsibility lies "the concept of perfection, the urge to conceive it, the intelligence to find a path towards it and the will to follow that path if not to the end, at least the distance needed to rise above individual limitation. . . . The quest for democracy in Burma is the struggle of a people to live whole, meaningful lives as free and equal members of the world community. It is part of the unceasing human endeavour to prove that the spirit of man can transcend the flaws of his nature.[20]

There were standing ovations after Alexander's speech, and hardly an eye was dry in the audience. The young man had touched the hearts of those assembled and, at night, thousands of Burmese—who had traveled to Oslo for the occasion—and others gathered outside the hotel on the capital's main street, Karl Johann Avenue, where he, his younger brother, Kim, and their father, Michael Aris, were staying. "We love Aung San Suu Kyi's family!" they chanted in unison. It was mid-December, cold and dark, and Karl Johann Avenue was bedecked in snow. They then marched in torchlight procession along the avenue. Santa Clauses, decorated fir trees, and stuffed reindeer adorned the shops along the route of the march, and the Burmese—seemingly oblivious of their unusual surroundings—shouted pro-democracy slogans in their native language.

The euphoria was understandable and it was a day of joy for the Burmese wherever they were. In Rangoon, the response was muted—no one dared to show in public what they felt. But in the privacy of their homes people celebrated. They lit candles and incense, and placed pictures of Suu Kyi beside Buddha images on the small altars that most Burmese families have in their homes. To many Burmese, the Nobel Peace Prize was more than an international recognition of her role as a political activist in the tradition of Mahatma Gandhi, Martin Luther King, and Nelson Mandela. In the minds of the Burmese, it attributed to her powers and qualities that went far beyond those of any ordinary political leader.

Her rise to fame—and near-sainthood—eventually became too much to bear even for SLORC chairman, Gen. Saw Maung. On December 17, he suffered a nervous breakdown, collapsed, and lost consciousness for more than half an hour.

The news spread quickly. After it was carried by the international media, other SLORC members apparently felt the need to respond by organizing stage-managed appearances for the ailing general. But wherever Saw Maung went, he looked dazed and battered, and the deterioration of his health became obvious on December 21, when he was invited to be the first to tee off at a tournament at the military golf course in Rangoon. In front of Burma's top brass and government officials, Saw Maung reportedly began screaming, "I am King Kyansittha!" Patting his holstered pistol, he warned onlookers to be "careful" or "I will personally kill you."[21]

His reference to one of the kings of the ancient Pagan empire was especially eccentric. Kyansittha, a powerful king whose name means "the remaining soldier" or "the one who was left behind," was the main character in a Moses-like story of a man who survived several attempts to kill him by rivals and enemies who wanted to take over the throne. Saw Maung, it was suggested at the time, may have seen himself as the only SLORC member who had also served as a minister in the pre-1988 BSPP regime.[22]

Astoundingly, Saw Maung's erratic performance was repeated in full view of the public exactly a month later when Burmese television showed him addressing a meeting with local SLORC officials. His rambling, incoherent speech also contained references to Kyansittha, the old regime, and various Buddhist scriptures. In the middle of the speech, Saw Maung exclaimed, "Today the country is being ruled by martial law. Martial law means no law at all." He concluded by telling the bewildered audience that "I always work with caution, perseverance, and wisdom. Wisdom does not mean black magic."[23]

It hardly came as a surprise when the Burma Broadcasting Service, on April 23, announced that Saw Maung had "been permitted to retire." He was succeeded by his deputy, Gen. Than Shwe, a taciturn, sullen officer with only very basic education at a village school in Kyaukse, a dusty town in the central plains. No one expected him to be a closet liberal but, to the surprise of many, he soon began releasing political prisoners, including former prime minister U Nu, who had been under house arrest since December 29, 1989. Suu Kyi's personal assistant, Ma Thanegi, who had been arrested during the crackdown in July of that year, was set free from Insein Prison. Even more startlingly, the SLORC announced that Suu Kyi's family would be allowed to visit her in Rangoon.

Some foreign observers were quick to come to the conclusion that Burma was close to some kind of breakthrough—but it was only the first of many cases of window-dressing aimed at appeasing the international community. In the end, nothing really changed. The National Convention first met on January 9, 1993, near the old British-built Kyaikkasan race course in Rangoon, but the meeting was adjourned after only two days. The emphasis, after all, was not on drafting a new constitution.

The junta's real intentions, which were to perpetuate its rule of the country and further bury the memory of the 1988 uprising and the military's subsequent humiliation in the 1990 election, became clear in a low-key announcement on September 15, 1993. The official media proclaimed the formation of the Union Solidarity and Development Association (USDA), a new organization whose aims were the same as those of the SLORC, "non-disintegration of national unity, perpetuation of sovereignty, and the promotion of national pride."[24]

Not surprisingly, its program, which was published in the official newspaper, *The New Light of Myanmar*—the new, internationally less objectionable name for the *Working People's Daily* since April of the same year—strikingly resembled that of the pre-1988 ruling party, the BSPP. Only references to "socialism" were missing. Following the disastrous performance of the BSPP's successor, the National Unity Party, in the 1990 election, it had become imperative for the military to build up a new "mass organization" to legitimize its rule by providing it with a civilian support base. But unlike the NUP, the USDA was not registered officially as a political party—it was and still is an "association"—so a new law that prevented civil servants from joining political parties does not apply to it.

Before long, reports indicated that many were signing up across the country. Special privileges were the main reason, or, as a Burmese citizen put it at the time, "If you're an USDA member, you get a passport easily, you can buy an air ticket without problem, and you get preference to jobs in the public sector."[25] With the core of the NLD crushed and its few remaining leaders cowed into submission, the USDA did not have to face any competition even if few people were joining it out of political conviction. The new SLORC chairman, Than Shwe, became the USDA's overall patron.

Then came the news that startled the world. At 4 p.m. on July 10, 1995, a delegation of military intelligence officers entered Suu Kyi's compound to inform her that the regime was "lifting the restrictions" that had been imposed on her on July 20, 1989.[26]

As night fell over Rangoon that day, the news had sped through the capital. A few foreign journalists, who had flown into Rangoon to cover what most expected to be a non-event—the sixth anniversary of her house arrest—suddenly found themselves in the midst of what at the time was believed to be the most dramatic change in Burma for several years. The foreign journalists and hundreds of Suu Kyi supporters gathered on University Avenue. The gate, which had been resolutely shut for almost exactly six years, was open. And there was a steady flow of people coming and leaving what had been the most well-guarded compound in Rangoon.

At first, the unexpected release raised hopes of national reconciliation—and Suu Kyi herself was also surprisingly conciliatory. She declared that she bore no grudge against the SLORC despite her long house arrest. And she called, once again, for a dialogue. "Once bitter enemies in South Africa are now working together for the betterment of their people. Why can't we look forward to a similar process?"[27]

But Burma's military rulers were no F. W. de Klerk, and the NLD could not be compared to the African National Congress. Nelson Mandela returned in February 1990 from his incarceration to lead a well-organized party. Suu Kyi had no similar structure to back her, crushed and cowed into submission as the remnants of the NLD were when she was released.

It soon became clear that the release of Suu Kyi was not the beginning of some political process leading to national reconciliation and genuine democratic reforms. Her release was not mentioned in the state-controlled media; instead, the *New Light of Myanmar* published a vitriolic attack on her husband, Michael Aris. A few months later, Tin Winn, Burma's then ambassador to Thailand, told the *Bangkok Post* that SLORC would not "discuss reform with Suu Kyi." Referring to the on-again, off-again National Convention, he argued that "as the process is going very smoothly, we don't need dialogue with anybody."[28]

Responding to these verbal attacks, in November the NLD withdrew its delegates to the National Convention—who, in any case, constituted only a handful of the 392 NLD candidates who had been elected in 1990. A few weeks later, the SLORC began attacking Suu Kyi directly, suggesting that she was a "traitor" and warning that she and her pro-democracy colleagues would be "annihilated" if they tried to "destabilize the country."[29]

The NLD of 1995 was no longer what it used to be. The unity among the pro-democracy forces—cherished by Suu Kyi and striking to everyone during the upheavals of 1988–89—was rapidly becoming a thing of the past. Arrests, torture, and constant intimidation of those who dared to continue the struggle were beginning to take their toll on her followers. The most high-profile pro-democracy activist to fall out with Suu Kyi was her once trusted personal secretary and close friend, Ma Thanegi. Having campaigned with Suu Kyi until the crackdown in July 1989, Ma Thanegi was sent to Insein Prison in Rangoon, where she spent nearly three years. Following Suu Kyi's release from house arrest, Ma Thanegi, however, chose not to follow the path of her old leader. She sparked a major controversy by writing a column in the *Far Eastern Economic Review* titled "The Burmese Fairy Tale" in which she attacked Suu Kyi's policies and methods.

> Like many Burmese, I am tired of living in a fairy tale. For years, outsiders portrayed the troubles of my country as a morality play: good against evil, with no shade of grey in between—a simplistic picture, but one the world believes. . . . But for us, Burma is no fairy-tale land with a simple solution to its problems.[30]

Ma Thanegi does not specify what the solution should be, but it appears that she thought that encouraging foreign aid and investment could result in the emergence of a more modern, and therefore also more democratic Burma.

> We had hoped that when [Suu Kyi] was released from house arrest in 1995 the country would move forward again. . . . [She] could have changed our lives dramatically. With her influence and prestige, she could have asked major aid donors such as the United States and Japan for help. She could have encouraged responsible companies to invest here, creating jobs and helping build a stable economy. She could have struck up a constructive dialogue with the government and laid the groundwork for a sustainable democracy. Instead, she chose the opposite, putting pressure on the government by telling foreign investors to stay away and asking foreign governments to withhold aid. Many of us cautioned her that this was counterproductive. Why couldn't economic development and political improvement grow side by side?[31]

Yes, why couldn't it? Ma Thanegi soon became the darling of the fledgling community of foreign investors who had flocked to the country in the wake of the "free-market" reforms and new foreign investment law that the junta had introduced after crushing the 1988 pro-democracy uprising. What could be more reasonable than a compromise, and who did not want to see Burma progress and develop, economically as well as politically?

Ma Thanegi was invited to address gatherings of policymakers and businessmen in the United States. But there she went even further in her criticism of Suu Kyi and of the West's Burma policies. Burmese politics, she said, "is an internal affair and foreigners should not get involved in it."[32]

Critics soon pointed out that it was not Suu Kyi who was opposed to a "constructive dialogue with the government," but the ruling junta, which consistently had refused to enter into any meaningful discussion with anyone outside its own inner circle. And as for encouraging "responsible companies to invest here, creating jobs, and helping build a stable economy," there was little Suu Kyi could do in that regard as long as the junta managed the economy as if it were a boot camp, issuing orders to private entrepreneurs and demanding bribes from every foreigner who arrived in the country to look into business opportunities.

Foreign investment in Burma soon began to dwindle, not as a result of calls for boycotts by the pro-democracy movement but because the military had created an environment in which no honest businessman could operate. Suu Kyi would have made a fool of herself if she had begun to encourage foreign companies to invest in Burma as long as the junta did not change its economic policies and curb widespread graft and corruption. Those were the real reasons why the Burmese economy never took off and why foreign investors were shunning the country.

Ma Thanegi's campaign against Suu Kyi was short-lived. She had been released ahead of the other political prisoners, which is always reason for believing that a "deal" had been made. When she began to appear as a columnist in the new English-language weekly *The Myanmar Times and Business Review*—a joint venture between an Australian businessman, Ross Dunkley, and high-ranking military intelligence officers—she became a pariah in the pro-democracy movement.[33] That was perhaps unfair. A kind of understanding may have been reached, not a "deal." There is nothing to indicate that Ma Thanegi received anything more than a certain freedom of movement and expression for writing her columns and for participating in international debates. But it is also beyond doubt that the junta considered Ma Thanegi useful, and therefore tolerated her activities, even if she occasionally also criticized the government.

At the same time, the situation inside the NLD continued to deteriorate. In December 1997, rumors had begun to circulate in Rangoon that Kyi Maung, the respected ex-army officer who had led the party to its election victory in 1990, had resigned because he disagreed with Suu Kyi's "confrontational stance against the government."[34] The NLD quickly denied the report, asserting that the eighty-year-old party activist was only "taking a rest because of his health."[35] But it was becoming increasingly clear that Suu Kyi's personality was part of the problem; she was stubborn, which was a strength, but as Kyi Maung had said, her single-mindedness was almost obsessive.[36]

On the other hand, her adversary, SLORC, showed no sign of relenting. It was digging in for the long haul, and not just to "restore law and order" following the "disturbances" of 1988. In November 1997, the junta was renamed the "State Peace and Development Council" (SPDC), indicating more permanent duties. If anyone had been in doubt as to what intentions the military had, it was now becoming clear that it had no intention to hand over power to the winners of the 1990 election, or to any other non-military entity.

Suu Kyi and her flock of remaining, faithful followers tried on a number of occasions to travel outside Rangoon to revitalize the movement but were repeatedly driven back. Then, in early 1999, Michael Aris was admitted to hospital in England for treatment for prostate cancer. On his deathbed, he had requested permission to visit his wife once more before dying. Appeals by several countries and organizations, including the pope and UN secretary general Kofi Annan, were made to the Burmese authorities to grant Michael a visa.[37] The SPDC responded by saying that Suu Kyi was free to travel to England to see him, but with no guarantee of her being permitted back into Burma again. Michael succumbed to his illness on March 27, his fifty-third birthday. Suu Kyi mourned in her home in Rangoon, now more lonely and isolated than ever.

The NLD was in a shambles. Ma Thanegi and Kyi Maung were not the only NLD, and former NLD, activists who found it difficult to work with Suu Kyi. In April 1999, a group of party workers broke ranks and issued a statement "calling for a new tack in dealing with the regime."[38]

The ringleader, forty-nine-year-old Rangoon businessman and MP-elect Than Tun, had opposed the decision to walk out of the National Convention in late 1995. Now, he and some of his associates called for low-level talks with the regime that excluded Suu Kyi. The idea was to break the deadlock, but they were promptly branded as traitors by the NLD leadership. A major mistake, it seems, was that they had sent a copy of their statement to military intelligence chief Khin Nyunt. Suu Kyi lashed out at the dissidents, "If you want to put suggestions to the NLD as loyal members, you don't address a copy to Khin Nyunt."[39]

Rather than initiating a bold political process, they found themselves expelled from the NLD—and being used against the party by the regime's propaganda machinery, which pounced on the internal conflict with glee and enthusiasm. At last, there was a serious split within the pro-democracy movement, which the regime could exploit to the hilt. It was becoming increasingly clear that there was no "middle way," that no compromise was possible on the strongly polarized political scene in Burma. Those who tried to make a stand in the middle soon found themselves crushed by both sides.

Likewise, foreign journalists, diplomats, and scholars who criticized Suu Kyi soon found themselves accused of opposing the pro-democracy movement in Burma as a whole. Barbara Victor, an American journalist and the author of a biography of Suu Kyi, points out that, "those people who are interested in Daw Suu Kyi as well as the overall political situation in Burma, whether they are writing articles or books or are students engaged in academic research, discover very quickly that there are precise rules that must be followed. . . . Any involvement or comment concerning the Burmese struggle for democracy should include only a condemnation of the SLORC. Deconstructing Aung San Suu Kyi is not part of the game."[40] In fact, any criticism of Suu Kyi is seen as "siding with the enemy." There is little or no room for a meaningful discussion about Suu Kyi's strengths and weaknesses.

The uncompromising nature of Burmese politics became even more evident when, in September 2000, Suu Kyi once again was placed under house arrest. She, NLD vice chairman Tin U, and a small following of party workers had tried to board a train to Mandalay only to find themselves under arrest. Suu Kyi had been escorted back to her home on University Avenue and not permitted to venture outside. It was never officially announced that she was back under house arrest, but she remained in her home for a year and a half, unable to communicate with the outside world. "Dialogue" and "national reconciliation" were not on the junta's agenda. It was determined to crush the NLD.

The only sign of any activity involving University Avenue came less than two months after her de facto detention. From his home in San Diego, California, her brother, Aung San U, filed a civil suit demanding half of their late mother's property, or the house in which Suu Kyi was staying. A court in Rangoon issued a subpoena to Suu Kyi, which she refused to accept. After three months of legal wrangling, Judge Soe Thein dismissed the suit in a rare show of defiance of the military authorities, who were doubtless behind the unusual and unexpected move. As a US citizen, Aung San U had no right to own or claim property in Burma. He tried subsequently to appeal the court's decision, but to no avail.

Suu Kyi's estranged brother had always been somewhat of an enigma. When the people first took to the streets in 1988, they had indeed hoped that he, the son of Aung San, would return from the United States to lead the struggle. But he hardly had the political acumen or the charisma of his sister, and he was soon ignored. It was only in December 1989—five months after his sister had been placed under house arrest—that he proclaimed himself "director of the Free Burma Front," an obscure organization with a limited following among Burmese exiles in the United States.

In February 1990, Aung San U published a mimeographed, forty-four-page booklet called "The Bridges to Freedom in Burma" that supposedly outlined a way forward for Burma's pro-democracy movement. It was a badly written piece of gibberish mixing scattered quotes from Thucydides, Napoleon, Winston Churchill, and the Upanishads with calls for the establishment of "community libraries and knowledge bases" as well as "physical fitness centers" for the general public. More intriguingly, Aung San U urged the Burmese to "beware of false leaders and phony prophets who are irresponsible and destructive. . . . They play upon the emotions of an undisciplined crowd. . . . We simply do not need these losers."[41]

It is unclear if this was a reference to his sister and the movement that she had initiated, but Aung San U fell silent after the NLD's 1990 election victory, only to resurface briefly a few years later to lay claim to the family property on University Avenue. At the time the court in Rangoon was considering it, enraged Burmese exiles staged several noisy rallies and protests outside his home in San Diego. He was not going to become a Burmese hero, or even a counterweight to his famous and revered younger sister.

International efforts to secure her release continued, and hopes were high when the UN in 2001 appointed Razali Ismail, a prominent

Malaysian diplomat, as the secretary general's new special envoy for Burma. Meeting government officials as well as NLD workers during several visits to Rangoon, he seemed to be making much more headway than any of his predecessors. Eventually, on May 6, 2002, Suu Kyi was freed after nineteen months of house arrest. A breakthrough appeared to be in sight, as government spokesman Col. Hla Min said the release would mark "a new page for the people of Myanmar (Burma) and the international community."[42]

As soon as she was released, Suu Kyi set out on a religious pilgrimage to meet U Vinaya, better known as Thamanya Sayadaw, a highly respected monk then residing on a mountaintop monastery near the Karen State capital of Pa-an. A strict vegetarian and devout Buddhist, he had been a staunch supporter of Suu Kyi for several years and was to be her main source of spiritual inspiration and guidance until his death at the age of ninety-three in November 2003.

Following the crackdown on the Buddhist *sangha* in 1990—and the arrest of scores of monks—the junta made a complete turnaround, proclaiming itself the upholder of religion and moral values. New, elaborate temples were built, and color TV sets, new cars, and other luxury items were bestowed on senior monks and abbots in exchange for their blessing and support.

One of the few who refused to be bribed in this manner was Thamanya Sayadaw. He repeatedly declined invitations to come to Rangoon to accept a new prestigious religious title that the junta wanted to give him, causing the authorities to finally come to his temple in eastern Burma to present the award.[43]

The hundreds of families that live around the monastery must still obey the rules of nonviolence and vegetarianism that the late abbot had introduced. There are also two schools in the vicinity where 375 children are taught by thirteen teachers, without books and other basic resources.[44]

Suu Kyi expressed her admiration for Thamanya Sayadaw in several of her "letters from Burma," which were published in the *Mainichi Daily* in 1995–96. "Whenever the *Hsayadaw* himself goes through his domain people sink down on their knees in obeisance, their faces bright with joy.

Young and old alike run out of their homes as soon as they spot his car coming, anxious not to miss the opportunity of receiving his blessing."[45] She apparently saw no contradiction between this religious worship and her political ideals.

> Some have questioned the appropriateness of talking about such matters as *metta* (loving-kindness) and *thissa* (truth) in the political context. But politics is about people and what we have seen in Thamanya proved that love and truth can move people more strongly than any form of coercion.[46]

In another of her "letters from Burma," she elaborated on the correlation of religion and politics.

> In my political work I have been helped and strengthened by the teachings of members of the *sangha* [Buddhist order of monks]. During my very first campaign trip across Burma, I received invaluable advice from monks in different parts of the country. In Prome a *Hsayadaw* told me to keep in mind the hermit Sumedha, who sacrificed the possibility of early liberation for himself alone and underwent many lives of striving that he might save others from suffering. So must you be prepared to strive for as long as might be necessary to achieve good and justice, exhorted the venerable *Hsayadaw*. . . . Of the words of wisdom I gathered during that journey across Burma, those of a ninety-one-year old *Hsayadaw* of Sagaing are particularly memorable. He sketched out for me tersely how it would be to work for democracy in Burma. "You will be attacked and reviled for engaging in honest politics," pronounced the *Hsayadaw*, "but you must persevere. Lay down an investment in *dukkha* [suffering] and you will gain *sukha* [bliss]."[47]

This highly spiritual approach to politics and social development marked, in fact, a major departure from her earlier writings, which had been far more down-to-earth and worldly. Before 1988, the main theme of her studies had been Burma's unfinished renaissance, how Burma—unlike India—had fallen short of achieving an East-West, new-old synthesis at the intellectual level. Now, she never mentioned the immaturity of Burma's political system or the shortcomings and weaknesses of Burmese social and intellectual structures. On the contrary, she began to use ancient Buddhist concepts and practices—*byama-so taya, metta, karuna, parami, sati, vipassana, nibbana, yahanda, bodhi*—in the fight for democracy.[48]

In many ways her "new" message came to resemble the philosophy of King Jigme Singye Wangchuk of Bhutan, whose private tutor Michael Aris had been in the 1970s. Rather than using the growth of his country's gross national product to measure progress, he introduced the concept of "gross national happiness," thus implying that spirituality is more important than economic growth. It is an open question to what extent this unusual approach to a nation's development has inspired Suu Kyi to preach similar concepts, but it is not inconceivable that it did, given the fact that she also spent several years in Bhutan in the 1970s.

According to Dutch Burma specialist Gustaaf Houtman, whose studies of Suu Kyi and Burma's "mental culture" stand out as some of the most valuable contributions to the understanding of Burmese life, society, and politics that have been produced in recent years:

> [These practices] inevitably lead to a personality cult from which she finds it difficult to extract herself. As the gap increasingly widens between the dirt and corruption represented by a repressive military regime and the purity and power of the heroic democracy fighters, so also the impersonal continuity of political organisations demanded by a truly democratic system is increasingly at risk.[49]

Houtman also argues that it was the many informal—and mostly mythical—stories of Suu Kyi's meetings with Thamanya Sayadaw that turned her into a saint and heroine in opposition to the regime. According to one such story, which is widely believed in Burma, Khin Nyunt also visited the *sayadaw*, but when he tried to start his car as he was leaving, he could not. He had to go back to the *sayadaw* and ask for help. The revered monk told the intelligence chief that when he stopped "being angry," his car would start. Finally, he was able to start his car. No such incident occurred when Suu Kyi visited the *sayadaw*.[50]

Many taxi drivers in Burma have photographs of Thamanya Sayadaw in their cabs for protection against accidents, but never of any of the Burmese generals. Suu Kyi has not done or said anything to enlighten the taxi drivers and others who believe in the supernatural powers of the *sayadaw*, and, by extension, in her. While this has made people rally behind her—and proved to the public that she is truly Burmese and not a "Mother of the West," as Hpe Kan Kaung and other crude propagandists for the regime claim—it has hardly led to a more modern approach to politics in a country where superstition has always been more important than rational thinking in the minds of most people.

Rather then being a bold reformer and modernizer, therefore, Suu Kyi has perhaps unwittingly risked becoming a conservative force, a "female Bodhisattva" that the people believe is going to deliver them from evil. This has no doubt made Suu Kyi even more popular with the public at large—or, rather, revered by them, as she is being perceived as somebody divine and sacred, a person who is much more than an ordinary human being. But it will not help pull Burma out of the Middle Ages, which is what the country really needs.

Admittedly, in her conversations with US Buddhist teacher Alan Clements, she denies that she has any nonworldly qualities or that she is an "extraordinary person," let alone a "female Bodhisattva."

> Do not think that I will be able to give you democracy. I will tell you frankly, I am not a magician. I do not possess any special power that will allow me to bring you democracy. I can say frankly that democracy will be achieved only by you, by all of you. By the will, perseverance, discipline, and courage of the people. As long as you possess these qualities, democracy will be achieved by you. I can only show you the path to democracy. That I can explain to you, from my experience learned from abroad and through research of my father's works done during his day.[51]

Although Suu Kyi often referred to her father, it was becoming increasingly clear to other observers that her policies and methods differed considerably from those of Aung San, a student radical, one-time Marxist, the "Bogyoke" (general) who had founded the Burmese army.

Rather, the influence of her mother, Khin Kyi, was becoming evident. Suu Kyi in her conversations with Clements emphasized, "I do try to be good. This is the way my mother brought me up. I'm not saying that I succeed all the time, but I do try."[52]

Suu Kyi's quest, as her son Alexander stressed in his speech in Oslo in 1991, is mainly spiritual, and that comes from her Buddhist mother and to some extent from her Christian maternal grandfather. By contrast, the father she never knew was a practical man, an orator, and a statesman who never mixed politics and religion. Had he lived, it is quite likely that Burma would have become a more modern society than it is today. Suu Kyi did not carry his policies forward; instead, her speeches, writings, and teachings—especially after her release from house arrest in 1995—are filled with Buddhist philosophy and Burmese popular beliefs, which seem to have little or nothing to do with the "unfinished renaissance" she had described and analyzed earlier. On the positive side, Suu Kyi had managed to mobilize the people of Burma against the military dictatorship, and through her many speeches across the country she had taught them about freedom and democracy. But her devotion to spiritualism was something new and harder for many to reconcile with. Combined with her personal stubbornness, it made her a difficult person to deal with.

This was an Aung San Suu Kyi who was very different from what she had written in her 1987 study *Burma and India: Some Aspects of Intellectual Life under Colonialism*, which, by contrast, described the limitations of Buddhist influence on life and society in Burma.

> Traditional Burmese education did not encourage speculation. This was largely due to the view, so universally accepted that it appears to be part of the racial psyche of the Burmese, that Buddhism represents the perfected philosophy. It therefore follows that there was no need either to develop it further or to consider other philosophies. . . . In India, besides the presence of a large minority of Muslims, Hinduism presented a far more diversified picture than Buddhism in Burma. . . . The Hindu world with all its rigid taboos was strangely flexible. It was in part this heritage of flexibility which

> enabled the Indian Renaissance thinkers to meet the challenge of British rule in intellectual and philosophical terms.[53]

The question now was whether Suu Kyi and what remained of the NLD—with all its spiritual baggage, and little or no political acumen and strategy—would be able to meet the challenge of military rule. In May 2003, Burma's dwindling pro-democracy movement was also jolted back to the brutal realities of the political system that the SLORC/SPDC had created, and which no amount of compassion or loving-kindness in the world could mollify.

During the year that had elapsed since she was released from house arrest on May 6, 2002, she had visited more than two hundred townships across the country, holding meetings and reopening NLD offices. Huge, enthusiastic crowds had come out to welcome her and her entourage even in small provincial towns. It was becoming clear to the junta that the pro-democracy movement was being restored, and therefore it had to be crushed once and for all.

The final showdown came on a country road near a remote town called Depayin northwest of Mandalay on May 30. In the morning, Suu Kyi and NLD vice chairman Tin U had paid homage to the abbot of the Zawtika monastery in Monywa, and left at about ten o'clock. Driving all day along a bumpy road, they reached the village of Kyi ten hours later. There were more than a hundred NLD activists accompanying Suu Kyi and Tin U in cars and on motorbikes.

Suddenly, they discovered that the road was blocked by thugs carrying "iron spikes and rods, bamboo batons, and wooden sticks."[54] Some were dressed in yellow robes, but wore white arm bands and did not behave like Buddhist monks. Then, the thugs attacked. Scores of NLD supporters and innocent bystanders—villagers who had come out to greet the entourage—were clubbed to death. The NLD women had their blouses and *longyi* stripped off and their heads bashed against the road. According to one eyewitness, "It was an evil act, brutal beyond belief, and the attackers acted with intent to kill. In addition, the attackers forcibly snatched gold chains, earrings, and money from the wounded."[55]

The attackers, who numbered some four thousand people—far more than would live in the vicinity of the place where the attack took place—spotted Suu Kyi's car and tried to ram it. Her driver was able to avoid a head-on collision with two heavy trucks blocking the road, and he plowed the car through three barbed wire barricades.

The carnage continued for more than three hours. Eyewitnesses later reported that, shortly after 11:00 p.m. that night, about eighty riot police and officers arrived at the scene of the attack. "Subsequently, two cars that appeared to be Mitsubishi Pajeros arrived. Two officious looking people got out of the cars and inspected the scene. The police . . . carted off the dead bodies in their Dybna trucks, as if they were throwing rubbish onto a garbage pile, and left the scene."[56]

It is unclear how many people were killed at Depayin, but eyewitnesses believe scores were clubbed to death and at least two hundred were injured, arrested, or missing.[57] Exact details were difficult to establish, because the authorities moved quickly to the location to destroy any evidence of a massacre. And many unsubstantiated rumors also circulated immediately after the incident. According to some initial reports, Suu Kyi had been badly hurt and Tin U killed. That, however, turned out to be an exaggeration. They were both relatively unscathed, but were taken into custody and escorted away from the scene.

The following day, the authorities announced that Suu Kyi had been taken into "protective custody" after clashes between her "supporters and pro-government protesters." The military authorities blamed the entire incident on the NLD, and claimed that it would have been no problem if "the NLD convoy could [have managed] to peacefully pass through the demonstrators on either side of the road and on the road."[58]

But who were the "demonstrators" who evidently had been trucked in for the attack, and who seemed well-organized and responded to orders shouted by somewhat older people who appeared to be officers? Investigations by Burmese advocacy groups as well as foreign diplomats in Rangoon, who traveled to the scene of the attack, soon established that it was the USDA, the Union Solidarity and Development Association, the junta's new mass organization led by SPDC chairman Than Shwe.

These fascist storm troopers, who had become known as the "White Shirts," an allusion to the Nazi "Brown Shirts" of the 1930s, were the new face of Burma's military dictatorship. The Depayin massacre was their first major physical attack on the pro-democracy movement. And it was clear the brutality had been effective. Suu Kyi was back under house arrest. There would be no more overt signs of any opposition to military rule until September 2007, when the country's Buddhist monks took to the streets to appeal for an end to the tyranny that has been gripping Burma for decades.

CHAPTER 4

THE "MYANMAFICATION" OF BURMA

March 27, Burma's Armed Forces Day, is meant to commemorate the day in 1945 when the Burmese nationalists, led by Aung San, shifted sides, joined the Allied powers, and took up arms against their former patron and benefactor, the Imperial Japanese Army. It used to be a day when army units marched down the streets of Rangoon chanting martial anthems and being garlanded by crowds of cheering well-wishers. After the 1988 massacres, however, military parades were held in secluded areas, away from a now potentially outraged public, but still in Rangoon.

Then came Armed Forces Day 2006, which was celebrated in an entirely different manner. Forgotten was the anti-fascist struggle in the past; even more importantly, the sixty-first Armed Forces Day was held at a vast, new parade ground in the new capital, Naypyidaw, near the old town of Pyinmana, which it is gradually absorbing. Only foreign defense attachés, not civilian diplomats, were invited, and they witnessed an amazing spectacle in the new "Capital of a King." The king in this case was Gen. Than Shwe, the leader of the ruling State Law and Development Council (SPDC), and Burma's new undisputed strongman following a series of unexpected purges in late 2004. Those purges involved the arrest and ouster of the military intelligence chief at the time, Khin Nyunt, who was also prime minister, along with up to thirty-five hundred intelligence personnel countrywide, including some three hundred senior officers.[1]

Khin Nyunt's fall from grace followed the death of his mentor, Gen. Ne Win, in December 2002. The old general had been placed under house arrest earlier that year, allegedly because of the corrupt behavior of his daughter, Sanda Win, her husband Aye Zaw Win, and the couple's three unruly grandsons, who had terrorized private businessmen in Rangoon with demands for bribes and "protection money." But few doubted that the move against Ne Win and his family came as preparation for the post-Ne Win era and to make sure that Khin Nyunt's influence would be limited. The dictator, who had ruled with an iron fist for several decades, was cremated near his home in Rangoon. The funeral was attended by a handful of family members and about twenty plainclothes military officers, none especially high-ranking.

Khin Nyunt's ouster was not, as some reports in the foreign media at the time suggested, a power struggle between the "pragmatic" intelligence chief and "hardliners" around Gen. Than Shwe and his deputy, Gen. Maung Aye. According to the press reports, Khin Nyunt favored a dialogue with long detained Suu Kyi and those opposed to the regime. Khin Nyunt had, after all, met her when she was under house arrest. Khin Nyunt may also have been smoother in his dealings with foreigners, but his dreaded military intelligence service, the DDSI, was the junta's primary instrument of repression against Suu Kyi's pro-democracy movement. During the August–September 1988 uprising, he had carried out Ne Win's orders, cracked down on the protesters, and had student activists imprisoned, tortured, and even killed.

A more plausible explanation for the purge was that Khin Nyunt and his DDSI had accumulated significant wealth through involvement in a wide range of commercial enterprises. They were building up a state within the state and not sharing their riches with the rest of the military elite. And Than Shwe did not want to have any potential rivals around him. Khin Nyunt clearly had political ambitions and he was not to be trusted.

Burmese military politics has always been murky, full of infighting and rivalries. As soon as one particular officer has become too rich and powerful, he is ousted. The only exceptions are Ne Win, who ruled from

1962 to 1988, and the present junta leader, Than Shwe, who has made himself a virtual monarch of the country.[2]

Than Shwe's path forward—indeed, his vision for his country—became clear on March 27 in Naypyidaw. Addressing a crowd of 12,000 soldiers, he said, "Our *Tatmadaw* [armed forces] should be a worthy heir to the traditions of the capable *tatmadaw* established by noble kings Anawratha, Bayinnaung, and Alaungpaya."[3] None of them had fought the Imperial Japanese Army, but Anawratha had in AD 1044 founded the first Burmese empire and established a new capital at the temple city of Pagan on the banks of the Irrawaddy River, southwest of today's Mandalay. He conquered Thaton, the capital of the Mon—major rivals of the Burmans for control of the central plains—and expanded his empire down to the Andaman Sea.

Bayinnaung was Burma's most celebrated warrior king. He reigned from 1551 to 1581 and conquered territories north of Pagan, parts of the Shan plateau in the east, and pushed as far east as Chiang Mai in today's northern Thailand and Vientiane in Laos. He was the most prominent ruler of the second Burmese empire and ruled from Pegu in the central plains.

Alaungpaya reigned in the eighteenth century and was the first king of the Konbaung dynasty, the third and last of the Burmese empires. Alaungpaya also fought the Mon, and his successor, Hsinbyushin, sacked the Thai capital of Ayutthaya in 1767, a deed for which the Thais have never forgiven the Burmese. But the Konbaung kings were defeated by the British in the three Anglo-Burmese wars of 1824–1826, and 1885, after which the country became a British colony. In 1885, Thibaw, the last king of Burma, was led away by the British in front of a mourning and wailing crowd who had come to bid farewell to the last monarch of an independent Burmese state. He was sent, with his once-powerful wife, Supayalat, and their children into exile in Ratanagiri in India, where he died in 1916.

On the Naypyidaw parade ground stand newly erected larger-than-life statues of the three warrior kings whom Than Shwe sees as his role models. He has also formed not only a new capital but a new Burmese state, the "State of Myanmar," a unitary state that is fundamentally different in nature from Aung San's concept of "unity in diversity," federalism, and some kind of parliamentary democracy. In "Myanmar" everybody is a "Myanmar" and the subject of the new king in Naypyidaw. There are no portraits of Aung San in Naypyidaw.

Some have argued that moving the country's capital was not unusual in an international historical context. Many countries have established purpose-built capitals away from major population centers, as Australia did when its government moved to the new city of Canberra in 1927—halfway between Sydney and Melbourne—or when, in the 1960s, Brazil built Brasilia, a new futuristic capital in the middle of the jungle far away from Rio de Janeiro and Sao Paulo. In more recent times, Nigeria moved its capital in 1999 to Abuja, a minor central town, from Lagos. In 1983, the small village of Yamoussoukro in central Ivory Coast was made the new capital, replacing Abidjan, one of West Africa's most bustling cities and commercial centers. Yamoussoukro had been chosen for only one reason: it was the home village of Félix Houphouët-Boigny, the then dictator of the Ivory Coast. Millions of dollars were spent on transforming Yamoussoukro into a new city, but it soon became the butt of jokes.

But Naypyidaw is no joke, nor is it comparable to Canberra or Brasilia. The construction of Burma's new capital was carried out in secret, and government officials were given only very short notice that they had to move. In November 2005, the Thailand-based *Irrawaddy* magazine reported:

> Diplomats, UN agencies and observers in Rangoon were dumb-founded to see hundreds of Chinese-made army trucks carrying officials, civilians and office supplies head north out of the capital. Neighbouring countries, Rangoon's diplomatic community and UN offices wanted to know how they were going to keep in touch with Burma's new centre of government. "Don't worry," they were told. "You can reach us by fax."[4]

According to one eyewitness:

> The area around Nay Pyi Daw was depopulated in order to seal the huge compound off from the outside world. Entire villages disappeared from

the map, their inhabitants driven off land their families had farmed for centuries. Hundreds—perhaps thousands—joined Burma's abused army of "internally displaced persons." Able-bodied villagers, however, were "enlisted" to help build the new capital.[5]

Apart from the parade ground with statues of the three kings, Naypyidaw now has a brand-new airstrip, a hospital, hotels—some reputedly five-star ones—military mansions, a new command center, government offices, and bunkers. Trucks that carried bricks, timber, and cement to Naypyidaw bore the logos of Burma's biggest construction companies, Htoo Trading and Asia World.[6] In May 2006, intelligence agencies in Thailand intercepted a message from Naypyidaw confirming the arrival of a group of North Korean tunneling experts at the site. Naypyidaw is at the foothills of Burma's eastern mountains, and it was becoming clear that the most sensitive military installations in the new capital would be relocated underground.[7]

The junta's apparent fear of a preemptive US invasion by sea or air strikes was at the time seen by some as a major motivation for the junta's decision to move the capital to what they perceived to be a safer, central mountainous location away from the coast. After all, the US government had publicly lumped Burma together with other rogue regimes and referred to it as an "outpost of tyranny."[8]

The *Irrawaddy* gave a more plausible explanation. The Burmese generals are less worried about a US invasion than they are of their own people. "Rangoon has never been a safe place for the paranoid generals. In 1989, when opposition leader Aung San Suu Kyi mobilized the people in the streets again, the regime declared Rangoon a war zone and assigned army officers and soldiers to deal with demonstrators."[9] Demonstrations, or any form of protest, are much less likely to take place in heavily fortified and secluded Naypyidaw, which also remains off-limits to most outsiders. It represented a safe place from which the country could be ruled without interference from "internal and external destructive elements," which is what the junta calls its domestic and foreign critics and opponents.

Military research centers, a new airport, as well as luxury private mansions for army officers, and especially family members who do not want to live in dreary Naypyidaw, have also been built in Pyin Oo Lwin, more commonly known as Maymyo, a former British hill station east of Mandalay, where the air is fresher and the scenery greener than in the dusty, gray central plains around Pyinmana.

At Naypyidaw, Than Shwe has founded his own royal city and founded a fourth Burmese empire in the spirit of Anawratha, Bayinnaung, and Alaungpaya. This is a far cry from the promises the junta gave when it assumed power on September 18, 1988: "The Defence Forces have no desire to hold on to power for a prolonged period."[10] Elections would be held, they had promised, and power handed over to the party that won the forthcoming elections. As "proof" of its temporary nature, the junta appointed only a small, nine-member caretaker cabinet.

Eighteen years later, though, the military is not only in power, but Than Shwe and his generals have reinvented the notion of what kind of state Burma is or should be. In this new state, there is no place for Aung San Suu Kyi or the National League for Democracy. They belong to Rangoon and the past. Than Shwe, the military, and Naypyidaw symbolize for them the future of a new royal state of Myanmar. The Armed Forces Day celebrations in 2006 were the ultimate proof of the military's desire to rule the country the way they believe is right, and to decide the destiny of its people.

The creation of a new national concept for Burma began when, on May 27, 1989, the official name of the country was changed to "Myanmar." "Burma," for reasons which are historically absolutely incorrect, was termed a "colonial name," and therefore had to be abandoned. But historical accuracy was not an issue for the generals. A Cultural Revolution had begun, and a military-appointed commission was appointed to rewrite Burmese history to suit the new power holders.

It was not only the country that was given a new, official name (although, as noted, it has always been *myanma naingngan* or *bama pyi* in Burmese). Rangoon became "Yangon," and there were even more offensive name changes in the ethnic minority areas, especially in Shan State. Pang Tara, Kengtung, Lai-Hka, Hsenwi, and Hsipaw—place names that have a meaning in Shan—have been renamed Pindaya, Kyaington,

Laycha, Theinli, and Thibaw, which sound Burmese but have no meaning in any language.[11]

Dutch Burma scholar Gustaaf Houtman calls this development the "Myanmafication of Burma," which he describes as a move away from the original idea of a federation—agreed by Aung San and the leaders of the ethnic minorities at the Panglong conference in February 1947—to the new "Myanmar" identity propagated by the junta.[12]

In an even more extreme attempt to show the supremacy of the "Myanmar race," in February 1997, the Burmese military sent an archaeological mission to northern Burma to look for fossils which they thought would prove that the human race actually originated in Burma, or, in their parlance, "Myanmar Naingngan." The Myanmar Fossil Exploration Team was supported by the Office of Strategic Studies, a military think-tank that Khin Nyunt controlled in Rangoon, and before the experts set off for the plains of northern Burma, Khin Nyunt stated:

> [It is] necessary to search for and uncover further incontrovertible evidence that the fossilised remains of higher primates found in Myanmar could be dated as being 40 million years old, in order to advance the studies into man's origins. The joint expedition teams of the Ministry of Defence and the geologists of the Ministry of Education . . . [are] being dispatched to search, explore and find such evidence. [Khin Nyunt] emphasised the fact that the mission of his team about to embark on this venture was of vital importance since it would greatly enhance the stature of the country in the world.[13]

A number of foreign experts, including paleontologists from the United States, France, and Japan joined in the jamboree, but nothing of any substance was found. They uncovered some bones and fossils, yes, but no evidence of a Myanmar super race, or that the earliest human beings originated in Burma. When Khin Nyunt was ousted in 2004, the fossil mission was quietly buried, although it is not inconceivable that Than Shwe would have liked to believe that the Myanmars were the first humans to walk on earth.

But whatever bones or artifacts dating back to the Stone Age or beyond were found, there is no proof that those had belonged to any "Myanmars" or "Burmans." Burma remains one of the most ethnically complex countries in the world. Officially, there are 135 "national races" in Burma, but that figure just points at another trait of the regime: a deep belief in astrology and numerology. 1+3+5 equals nine, and nine was Ne Win's, and also the army's, lucky number, which also symbolizes fulfillment and unity. The army was also founded on March 27—2+7=9.[14]

A more realistic estimate of the number of ethnic groups in Burma would be thirty to forty—a considerable number in a country of less than fifty million people. They all speak different languages, which makes the concept of "Myanmar" even more difficult to understand. If Burma meant only the central plains, and Myanmar the Burmans and all the other nationalities, how could there be, according to the Myanmar Language Commission, a "Myanmar language"? The commission's latest "Myanmar-English Dictionary" also mentions a "Myanmar alphabet." Clearly, there is no difference between "Burmese" and "Myanmar." The Myanmar language is the Burmese language, nothing else. Burma and Myanmar (and Burmese and Myanmar) mean exactly the same thing, and it cannot be argued that the term "Myanmar" includes any more people within the present union than the name "Burma" does.

No authoritative history of the many peoples of Burma and their origin has ever been written, but most historians—though, not the SPDC—accept the theory that the present inhabitants of the central Burmese plains migrated from the north in different waves about a thousand years ago. They then clashed with the indigenous peoples of the region, the Mon, who had their own kingdoms and literature, and the Karen, a hill people without any written account of their early history. The Burmans adopted Buddhism from the Mon and learned their alphabet, which was modified and used to write Burmese.[15]

Many Mon were assimilated into the new Burmese kingdoms and empires, but the Karen suffered more at the hands of the aggressive Burman invaders than any other people in the region. They were treated as inferiors and, unlike the Mon, discouraged from intermingling with the Burmans. When Christian missionaries arrived at Burma's coasts in the early nineteenth century, many Karen converted—and later fought with the British against the Burmans in the Anglo-Burmese wars. During the colonial era, they served with the British police and army, and they fought the Japanese during World War II. A Karen army has been fighting for independence or autonomy since Burma's independence, and they are still fighting in the hills of eastern Burma. So have their brethren to the north, the Karenni, a subgroup of the Karen, who the Burmese call Kayah, hence "Kayah State."

Besides the Karen, the Shan are the most numerous of Burma's many ethnic groups, and they are not related to any other ethnic group in Burma. The word "Shan" is actually a Burmese corruption of "Siam" or "Syam"; the letter "m" becomes "n" as a final consonant in Burmese. Because of their closeness to the Thais, and their history of independent principalities, there has been little loyalty to the Burmese—or Myanmar—state from the Shan. A Shan rebellion for independence broke out in 1958 because they were not granted the right to secede after a ten-year period of independence, a right they had under Burma's first, 1947, constitution. The Shan rebellion continues to this day.

But an independent Shan State would face the same problem with ethnic minorities as Burma: only 60 percent of its population of approximately seven million people are Shan. The rest are Kachin, Wa, Lahu, Palaung, Padaung, Pa-O, and other hill tribes, as well as ethnic Chinese in the Kokang area in the remote northeastern corner of the state. Burma's 40-percent-minority population are not happy to belong to Burma—or to be called "Myanmars"; nor would the 40 percent of the population of Shan State who are not Shan accept rule by the Shan. In fact, the Pa-O rebellion, which broke out in the early 1950s, was an uprising against the Shan princes, or *saohpas*.

The Kachin speak Tibeto-Burman languages—altogether at least seven different tongues—but adopted Christianity more than a century ago. The missionaries put their main language, Jingphaw, into Roman script, and thus the Kachin got their own written language and literature. And they, too, have been waging a war for their independence. A Kachin uprising broke out in the Kachin-inhabited areas of Shan State in 1961, and then spread to Kachin State proper.

Akin to the Kachin are two other Tibeto-Burman tribes in the northwest, the Naga and the Chin. Like the Kachin, the Chin were animists until the arrival of Christian missionaries in the late nineteenth and early twentieth centuries. The latter put the Chin dialects into written form as well, using the Roman alphabet. Neither the Kachin nor the Chin hills were ever fully conquered by the Burman kings, and they maintained their independence until the British colonial power arrived. Even then, rule over their areas was light and indirect; the village chiefs were left to rule local communities, as long as they remained loyal to the colonial power and supplied it with men for the police force and the army. On the eve of World War II, only 1,893 of the soldiers of the colonial army were Burmans, compared to 2,797 Karen, 2,578 Indians, 1,258 Chin, and 852 Kachin.[16]

The Naga inhabit the remote mountain regions near the Indian frontier in the northwest. While the Naga tribes on the Indian side of the border were converted to Christianity at about the same time as the Kachin and Chin, and obtained their own Roman script as well, the Naga on the Burmese side lived in isolation. These Burmese Naga were headhunters into the 1970s and perhaps even the 1980s—no one knows for sure—and were feared by the plains people.

South of the Naga and Chin hills lies the Arakan region, which had been a separate and politically advanced kingdom until it was conquered by the Burmans in 1784. The Arakanese language is an earlier, archaic form of Burmese and the features of the Arakanese reflect their origin. They look like a mixture of people from the Indian subcontinent and Mongols. Most Arakanese are Buddhist like the Burmans, but there is a large Muslim minority living in the west, near the border with Bangladesh. They speak the Chittagonian dialect of Bengali and call themselves Rohingya. The Buddhist Arakanese call them illegal immigrants from Bangladesh, although there has been a Muslim population in the area for at least three hundred years.

During the colonial period, the British brought in Indians to work in the civil service, and for the railways and the telegraph. Most of them returned to India either after independence or after Ne Win's coup in

1962. Many remained, though, and there are Indian as well as Chinese merchants and laborers in most Burmese cities and towns.

All this is "Myanmar." It would be a nightmare for any government to forge some kind of national unity from these diverse ethnic groups, who were only forced to live under the same roof on the advent of British colonialism. The concept of the military junta—"we are all Myanmars"—may thus appear offensive to the ethnic minorities and absurd to international historians. According to Houtman:

> When I observed [cultural] performances in 1979, each ethnic group rose onto the stage as a separate entity in its own right, in their own costumes, dancing their own dances, and singing their own songs in their own language. Even if it meant little at government level, at least the idea of cultural uniqueness of the different groups was preserved in this contrived performance. However, when I watched Burmese national television in June 1998, ethnic groups were being subordinated to a new overarching concept of Myanmar culture, for all combined to dance the same dance, [wave] the same Burmese flag, sing the same song in the same Burmese language, under the frequent chorus of "Us Myanmar." The only permissible differentiating characteristic was a different costume colour for each ethnic group.[17]

Yet the NLD's reference in its September 1988 manifesto to "the tragedy" of ethnic relations in Burma is also inadequate and unlikely to solve Burma's ethnic problems, as is Suu Kyi's statement in Myitkyina in 1989: "We cannot have the attitude of 'I'm Kachin,' 'I'm Burman,' 'I'm Shan.' We must have the attitude that we are all comrades in the struggle for democratic rights."[18]

With Suu Kyi back under house arrest, and the NLD reduced to a gathering of geriatrics, even that struggle for democracy had been effectively strangled. Meanwhile, Than Shwe and the SPDC continued to strengthen their pillar of support, the Union Solidarity and Development Association (USDA). Apart from its "Three National Causes"—"non-disintegration of the Union, non-disintegration of national solidarity, and perpetuation of sovereignty"—it also articulated in its own inimitable phraseology a "Four-Point People's Desire: "oppose those relying on external elements, acting as stooges or holding negative views; oppose those trying to jeopardize the stability of the State and progress of the nation; oppose foreign nations interfering in internal affairs of the State; and crush all internal and external destructive elements as the common enemy."[19]

The USDA became the vehicle for the SPDC's recreation of civil society while suppressing all other alternative possibilities, especially in areas inhabited by ethnic minorities. It established offices at national, district, township, and about one in four ward or village levels.[20] By 1997, the USDA claimed to have 7.51 million members, which rose to 10 million in 1998, and 22.8 million in 2005, or nearly half the population of Burma.[21] Now, its mass rallies are attended by up to a hundred thousand people, all proclaiming their allegiance to the new State of Myanmar and its National Convention, which is supposed to draw up the country's new constitution.

In recent years, the USDA has also assumed a paramilitary role in society. Official media has described it as "a reserve force for national defence," which has trained "2,395 new generation air youths and 2,614 new generation naval youths."[22] Than Shwe himself, the senior patron of the USDA, had stressed already in 1996 at an "Executive Advanced Management Course" organized by the USDA that

> the trainees constitute not only the hard core force of the USDA, but also the sole national force which will always join hands with the *tatmadaw* [armed forces] to serve national and public interests. Hence . . . they should be morally and physically strong with sharp national defence qualities. Therefore . . . the trainees will be taught military parade, military tactics, and the use of weapons.[23]

Basic military training has become part of the USDA's policy of mass mobilization, and it has also formed its own militia forces, especially in ethnic minority areas. These have taken on names such as "the Anti-Foreign Invasion Force," "the State Defense Force," and "the People's Strength Organization." As early as 1997, army chief and deputy SPDC chairman, Gen. Maung Aye, referred to the USDA as an "auxiliary national defence force," thus acknowledging its security role in the country.[24]

With the sacking of intelligence chief Khin Nyunt in 2004 and the purging of all his associates, the USDA has also assumed an intelligence function. According to a report on the USDA compiled by the Thailand-based Network for Democracy and Development:

> The SPDC has met with USDA central executive committee members and other loyal members to train them as intelligence officers, forming intelligence teams in each township. One intelligence team in Mon State adopted responsibilities which included watching the NLD as well as other members of the opposition. All information collected was expected to be reported directly to the USDA general headquarters.[25]

The same report stated that, in December 2005, a USDA meeting was held in which members were instructed to "watch all army and police forces including staffs from various departments within the township" and report to headquarters.[26] In other words, USDA members are being used not only to watch the opposition, but to monitor the actions of the regime's other institutions.

Consequently, according to Houtman, a culture of violence and intimidation has come to surround this new, mighty mass organization, which is "designed in particular to frighten and deter NLD members, their supporters, and residents in their neighborhood. With an active USDA the regime hopes that NLD political activity will be curtailed, once NLD visitors or NLD elements are known to automatically attract USDA 'volunteers' intent on wreaking havoc to disrupt proceedings."[27]

When Suu Kyi was still able to give interviews to foreign reporters, she told American journalists Leslie Kean and Dennis Bernstein:

> The USDA is increasingly becoming a branch of the local authorities. On Burmese New Year's Day [1997] the USDA people were sent over to my house to physically break up the NLD . . . at a fish-releasing ceremony. In another incident, members of the USDA, most of them students, were instructed to throw tomatoes at me at the anniversary of the death of

> Burma's first democratic prime minister [U Nu]. . . . Sadly many students are members of the USDA because they're forced to be, partly through threats. In some schools, they are threatened that if they don't become a member of the USDA, they will not be allowed to take their examination, or they will not be given good grades. I received a letter from a teacher who said that in her school those who want to go to their classes reserved for the best students have become members of the USDA, so students must join for their own survival.[28]

And, Suu Kyi warned, the USDA was not to be dismissed as just another farcical invention by the junta:

> The world community must realise that the USDA is not an innocent social-welfare organisation, as it claims to be, but an organisation being used by the authorities as a gang of thugs. Their operations resemble those of the Nazi Brown Shirts. The [junta] sent people from a so-called welfare organisation to beat up people taking part in a non-violent, religious ceremony. I must say that that amounts to something very, very close to what the Brown Shirts used to do in Germany.[29]

Suu Kyi herself became the target of USDA violence in Depayin in May 2003, which also led to a renewed spell of house arrest. Given the coercion involved in recruiting members for the USDA, it is questionable whether its foundations are any stronger than the erstwhile Burma Socialist Programme Party, which collapsed like a pack of cards in 1988. The difference is that the USDA, unlike the BSPP, is not the only legally permitted political organization in the country. One of the stated objectives of the USDA, which was outlined in a secret document in 2004, is "narrowing and eliminating the activities of opposition forces . . . [and to] diminish and ruin the opposition parties' capacity economically."[30]

Unlike the BSPP, the USDA has also carved out a role for itself in the Burmese economy, enabling the SPDC to control and manipulate the new, ostensibly free-market-oriented economy that was introduced after the upheavals of 1988. The USDA's main business front is the Myangonmyint Company; it also controls the local gem market and the investment firm

Myanmar Economic Holdings. In 1995, the USDA obtained control over the Panlong Yadana and Theingyi markets in Rangoon; it runs bus and train lines and car rental services; it collects taxes and is involved in housing and real estate, fishing, paddy cultivation, rice milling, transportation of cement and construction materials, and supply of water; and it imports cars, motorcycles, and spare parts into the country free of tariffs.[31]

Furthermore, the USDA has reached out to parties and organizations in other parts of Asia, claiming to represent "the people of Myanmar." In 2000, the Communist Party of China—China being a close ally of the SPDC—invited Gen. Win Myint to Beijing, not in his role as one of the top generals in the junta, but in his capacity as USDA vice president. Four years later, the Chinese communists invited eighty-four political parties, including the USDA, from thirty-five countries to the "Third All Asian Parties Forum" held in Beijing. Members of the USDA have participated in an International Youth Development Exchange Programme in Tokyo, and in January 2006 representatives of the organization attended the Third Asia Pacific Regional Cuba Solidarity Conference in India. And when Malaysian foreign minister Syed Hamid Albar visited Burma in March 2006 as an envoy for the Association of Southeast Asian Nations (ASEAN), he met with officials from the USDA, but not with anyone from the NLD or other opposition parties.[32]

In Burma today, it is almost impossible for any citizen to survive and prosper without being a member of the USDA. The SPDC's and USDA's emphasis is given to the youth in "what it may regard as a long-term approach to ensuring its continuing role into the next generation," to quote US Burma expert David Steinberg, who also stresses that the USDA will remain important "only insofar as the military have an active role in governance. After all, the youth movements of the BSPP were ephemeral as well."[33]

Larry Jagan of *Asia Times Online* commented in June 2006:

> The reality is that the popularity of Suu Kyi—and the National League for Democracy she founded—still widely outpaces the ruling junta's, whose illegitimate rule has run the economy into the ground and placed the

> country's democratic hopes behind bars. Across the country, Suu Kyi is affectionately referred to simply as "the Lady."[34]

The military, supported by the USDA, is likely to remain in power for the foreseeable future, though, and there is precious little Suu Kyi, despite her popularity, can do about it from her home on Rangoon's University Avenue, cut off from her supporters and isolated from the rest of the world. She has nevertheless remained a symbol of defiance and moral strength, and, as such, has attracted sympathy and support not only inside Burma but from all over the world. In September 2004, artists including U2, Eric Clapton, Paul McCartney, Natalie Merchant, Sting, Pearl Jam, Peter Gabriel, Damien Rice, and Ani DiFranco even recorded an album dedicated to Suu Kyi and "the courageous people of Burma." Bono of U2 declared that "Aung San Suu Kyi is a real hero" and "a modern icon of moral courage."[35] Eric Clapton said that "anytime anyone inside Burma listens to my music, I want them to know that they are listening to an artist that supports their freedom."[36]

The SPDC, however, could not care less, and Suu Kyi's nemesis, Than Shwe, continued to quietly consolidate his grip on power. The sullen and slow-moving general has surprised many by his determination to reshape Burma's future and his role in it. When in April 1992 he took over from Saw Maung as chairman of the junta, no one expected much of him. Born in the central town of Kyaukse in 1933, he worked for a while in a post office before joining the army at the age of twenty. In 1958, he was attached to the psychological warfare department, but was posted back to the army a few years later.

He was immensely loyal to Ne Win as long as the old strongman was in power, and that ensured him a rapid rise through the ranks. In 1978 he was promoted to colonel, and at fifty he became one of the youngest regional commanders in the Burmese army when he took over the Southwest Regional Command. Than Shwe later served at the frontline against the insurgent Communist Party of Burma (CPB) in eastern Shan State. He became a central executive committee member of the BSPP in 1988, and deputy head of the State Law and Order Restoration Council, the first junta, in September of that year.

According to Burmese journalist Aung Zaw, Than Shwe and his wife, Kyaing Kyaing, an ethnic Pa-O from Mon State, were "unusually modest" for an army couple. When going to school, their children "would ride an army truck instead of the luxury sedans that transported other generals' kids."[37] And despite his limited education, he reads a lot, mostly books on politics and science. He does not speak or read English, but has his aides translate articles from international magazines such as *Time*. When not reading, he plays golf with other army officers. However, Than Shwe is deeply superstitious and regularly seeks advice from famous Burmese astrologers before making any major political decisions. One of them is E Thi, or ET as she is known, a disabled woman whose speech makes her virtually incomprehensible. Her sister translates ET's blurry prognostications for those seeking her counsel.[38]

At BSPP meetings in the past, Than Shwe would "often subject his audiences to blather," Aung Zaw asserts. Whenever he gave a speech, it could go on for several hours, "but he really never said anything." His economic policies turned out to be as dull and equivocal as his speeches. While his rival, Khin Nyunt, had tried to be modern, encouraging Burma's integration into the global economy by promoting "e-business," Than Shwe champions dams and agricultural projects without any real purpose. He has also developed his hometown, Kyaukse, into an industrial zone, and, of course, he built a new capital at Naypyidaw.

Some private businessmen have prospered under Than Shwe's patronage. The mightiest of them is Tay Za, who is only in his forties but is managing director of the Htoo Trading Company, one of Burma's biggest conglomerates. Apart from being involved in the construction of Naypyidaw, Htoo Trading is also a major player in many other businesses ranging from tourism and the hotel trade to arms imports. Tay Za also set up another company, Myanmar Avia Export, which became Burma's sole representative for the Export Military Industrial Group of Russia, and of the Russian helicopter company Rostvertol. According to the *Irrawaddy*, for he was instrumental in the junta's purchase of advanced MiG-29 fighter-bombers and helicopters from Russia.[39]

Hardly surprisingly, Tay Za is a close friend of Kyaing San Shwe, Than Shwe's son. Tay Za sealed that friendship by buying him a US-made

Hummer, the civilian version of the military Humvee, the only one of its kind in Rangoon. But he and the general's family strongly deny persistent rumors that he is involved with one of Than Shwe's daughters.[40]

Tay Za might be the wealthiest of Than Shwe's cronies, but he is not the only one. Other cronies include Tun Myint Naing, also known as Steven Law, the managing director of the company Asia World and the son of retired opium warlord Lo Hsing-han; and Eike Htun, a former truck driver who formed the Asia Wealth Bank and has also been linked to Burma's drug trade. Another banker with shady connections, Aung Ko Win of the Kanbawza Bank, is closer to Gen. Maung Aye, the vice chairman of the Burmese junta. Without military connections in one form or another, it is not possible to prosper in Than Shwe's kingdom.

Than Shwe's power structure is rather simple. Apart from being SPDC chairman and thus de facto head of state, he is also commander-in-chief of the military, the only real power center in today's Burma. The armed forces have expanded rapidly since the 1988 uprising, probably to ensure that their supremacy should not be challenged by another popular uprising. Prior to the upheavals, the three services of the armed forces—the army, navy, and air force—totalled approximately 185,000 men. By 2006, they were more than 400,000, at the same time as the junta actually had managed to reach cease-fire deals with more than twenty insurgent groups in the country's border areas. Among these were the offshoots of the CPB—which in 1989 broke up into four different ethnic armies, of which the United Wa State Army is the strongest—and the once powerful Kachin Independence Army (KIA) in the far north of the country.

More than a billion dollars have been spent on arms purchases, mainly from China, at a time when Burma had no external enemies and the decades-long civil war was coming to a halt. China has supplied tanks, army trucks, artillery pieces, airplanes, naval patrol boats, anti-aircraft guns, and light weaponry. Burma has also procured howitzers from India, tanks from Ukraine, mortars from Pakistan, artillery pieces from North Korea, and assorted weapons and military equipment from Israel, Russia, Serbia, and Singapore. Never before has Burma had such powerful—and well-equipped—armed forces, and the build-up was clearly meant to secure the military's grip on power and to make sure that there would be no repeat of the popular uprising of 1988. There is no shortage of countries that are willing to sell weapons to the Burmese generals, despite stiff sanctions and arms embargoes imposed by the US and the European Union.

To remain in power the military has made sure that the constitution the National Convention has been working on for years includes clauses that will give the armed forces a dominant role in the decision-making process as well as the governance of the country. At the end of January 2006, the official newspaper, *The New Light of Myanmar*, reported that the Convention had approved "thirteen clauses related to the military."[41] Military men (there are no women in the armed forces) will occupy a minimum of 25 percent of the seats in any future parliament, and the armed forces will be "allowed to encroach on any part of the country should an ill-defined 'calamity' occur."[42] Also included is the provision that the chief of the armed forces will automatically serve as vice president of the country. "National reconciliation," advocated by the NLD and Burmese groups in exile, is not part of Than Shwe's plans for Burma's future. The official media prefer to refer to the ongoing process as "national reconsolidation."[43]

To consolidate the nation, numerous "destructive elements" have been incarcerated, tortured, and killed. One of the first and most prominent was Ba Thaw, a former naval officer who later became a writer under the pen name Maung Thaw Ka. He left the navy after being involved in a shipwreck in 1956. When the ship was sinking, he and twenty-six other naval personnel transferred to two inflatable life rafts. One raft was lost with all nine passengers on board, but the other was rescued by a Japanese ship twelve days later. By then, seven of the eighteen men were dead and one died on the rescue ship. Maung Thaw Ka wrote a gripping, best-selling book about the ordeal. He also translated William Cowper's *The Solitude of Alexander Selkirk* from English into Burmese as well as poems by Shakespeare, Herrick, Donne, and Shelley.[44]

But Maung Thaw Ka was an unusually outspoken critic of the BSPP and joined the uprising in 1988, and that became his downfall. It is said that he was instrumental in persuading Suu Kyi to appear in public on August 26 of that year, which marked the beginning of her political activities. Maung Thaw Ka was also one of the founders of the NLD and chairman of its branch in Sagaing Division.

He was arrested in 1989 and sentenced to twenty years' imprisonment for urging his old comrades in the navy to join the pro-democracy movement. He suffered from spondylitis before he was arrested, and his condition deteriorated after maltreatment in prison. The prison authorities also denied him medication, and as a result he suffered a severe heart attack and died in June 1991 at the age of sixty-five.[45]

Another prominent personality who died because of ill-treatment in jail was Leo Nichols, a Burmese of partly Greek origin. He served as honorary consul for Norway in 1969, was appointed honorary consul for Denmark in 1978, and also informally represented Finland and Switzerland in Rangoon. Nichols was also Suu Kyi's godfather and close to her and her family. He was arrested in April 1996 and charged with operating a fax machine and phone lines "without official permission."[46] In reality, Suu Kyi was using his fax machine to send her articles to the *Mainichi Daily* in Japan, and letting her do that was, in the eyes of the junta, a serious crime. He suffered from diabetes, hypertension, and heart problems, and, like Maung Thaw Ka, was denied medication. He was also forced to stand up for hours during his interrogations, sometimes in the middle of the night. Eyewitnesses say his legs were "visibly swollen and he couldn't walk properly."[47]

On June 22, Nichols died in prison while waiting for an appeal. The authorities claimed that he died from "eating food he should not have taken."[48] He was buried in a cemetery in Rangoon the day after his death. No autopsy was conducted and because of the haste of the burial, none of his family members was able to be present at the funeral. Amnesty International issued a statement calling on the authorities to provide a detailed explanation of how Nichols was treated while in detention.[49] Needless to say, there was no response from Rangoon.

Other, lesser known pro-democracy activists also died in prison, among them Aung May Thu, a sixty-one-year-old NLD member from Minhla who was arrested in 1989 and sentenced by a military tribunal to ten years' imprisonment. He died in Tharrawaddy prison on September

17, 2002. Aye Mu, a twenty-one-year-old woman in Thayetchaung township in Tenasserim Division, was arrested and raped by military men in September 1997. She was then sentenced to five years' imprisonment for political activities, tortured and raped again, and as a result died in Tavoy prison in May 1998.[50]

On August 2, 1996, Hla Than, an NLD member of parliament elected in 1990, died in Rangoon General Hospital, to which he had been transferred from his prison cell for "treatment." Hla Than was arrested in 1991, and accused of "complicity in attempts to set up a parallel government."[51] A martial law court sentenced him to twenty-five years' imprisonment for high treason. His main crime, perhaps, was that it was he who had won the election on Coco Islands, the country's smallest constituency, but one of the best known because of its naval base and the absence of civilians. Hla Than's death certificate stated that he had died of "extensive Koch's lung [tuberculosis] and HIV infection." Suu Kyi wrote about his death in one of her letters from Burma:

> Coincidentally on the day of his death, extracts from a report on conditions in Burmese prisons by a student activist who had served time in the infamous Insein Jail, where U Hla Than was incarcerated for nearly six years, appeared in the *Nation* newspaper of Bangkok. The report states that owing to drug abuse "there is . . . a high prevalence of HIV/AIDS in prisons. When administering injections, the doctors only give half or less than half of the phial to one patient, giving the rest to another patient from the same needle and syringe, almost guaranteeing that any blood-carried infections will spread." There can be little doubt that U Hla Than's death was brought about by the abysmal prison conditions that do not bear scrutiny by independent observers.[52]

Khin Maung Myint, a forty-two-year-old NLD worker, died on July 21, 2001, as a result of mistreatment in Kale prison in northeastern Burma, which is notorious for poor facilities and insufficient food. Ko Oo was sixty-four when he died in Thayet prison on March 23, 2006. Min Thu, a lawyer and member of the NLD, was arrested in 1998 and died on June 13, 2004. He suffered from hypertension, heart disease, and a bulbous growth on his bones, and was denied proper medical care. Oo Tha Tun, a pro-democracy activist from Arakan State, was arrested in March 1990. He was then eighty-two years old, and died five months later, also deprived of medicine and medical care.

Myint Than, a fifty-six-year-old Shan political leader, was arrested in February 2005 and sentenced to seventy-nine years in jail for forming a Shan advisory group to assist Shan MPs who were elected in May 1990, which authorities said amounted to encouraging an insurrection against the state. Myint Than was in good health when he was sent to Sandoway prison in Arakan State, but died in May the following year. He suffered from chest pain and had had a stroke for reasons that are not entirely clear. Most likely, he had been severely tortured.

Many more just disappeared in Burma's notorious prisons, their families never told about their fate. Other political prisoners have perished in the country's labor camps. Political prisoners are often forced to work on the regime's many "development projects." According to the Assistance Association for Political Prisoners, a Thailand-based NGO, "On-site accidents are common due to the nature of the work being done (building roads, breaking rock, portering). Many have been left to die without any effort made to inform that individual's family."[53] One former political prisoner recalls:

> They sent me to a hard labour site to carry full water tanks. They were very heavy. I was there for three days, and demanded that the jail officer release me from work because of my age; I was 36 years old. Most of the people at this work camp were 16 or 17 years old. But, if they want you to work, age is not an issue. They will force 60 and 70 year olds to work. At this camp, there are many people over 50.[54]

Political prisoners are routinely punched, kicked, slapped, kneed, and beaten with a variety of implements, including rubber or wooden batons, truncheons, rifle butts, rubber cords, bamboo sticks, and plastic pipes. According to the Assistance Association for Political Prisoners, "The authorities beat all parts of the prisoner's body, including the head, and generally target places where a prisoner is already injured."[55] There are several positions that political prisoners have been forced to assume while being beaten. The more common positions are said to be standing and holding on to a post, lying on the floor of the cell, crawling on the ground, sometimes while in heavy iron shackles, squatting and standing continuously, and being forced to perform squat-jumps, as in the game of leap-frog. Female prisoners are often sexually abused.

Even for those who are released, their sufferings do not end when they leave prison, as a former political prisoner explains.

> Political prisoners also faced psychological torture while in prison. When released, they must attempt to rebuild their identity. They are often turned away from universities and jobs. If they do find work, they remain under the constant watch of the Military Intelligence. Their family and friends are watched as well, leading to an end to many relationships. The difficulty of reintegrating into society has further exacerbated mental suffering. In Burma, rehabilitation and counselling services are not offered, and there is a stigma attached to those with mental illness. As a result, former political prisoners do not address their psychological problems, and a few have subsequently committed suicide.[56]

Than Shwe's new State of Myanmar has become even more repressive than Burma ever was under the old dictator, Ne Win. Although the United Nations as well as nongovernmental organizations such as Amnesty International and Human Rights Watch have repeatedly condemned human rights abuses in Burma, and the International Labour Organization has urged the authorities to stop using forced labor on development projects, Than Shwe and his regime show no sign of relenting. Repeated appeals for a dialogue with the NLD and other oppositions groups have also fallen on deaf ears. There is no room for compromise in Than Shwe's kingdom.

Offers of international mediation, or attempts at persuading the dictatorship to be more conciliatory, have also failed miserably. In March 2003, a UN human rights envoy, Paulo Sergio Pinheiro, cut short his mission to Burma when he discovered a hidden microphone under a table during what was supposed to be a private meeting with a political prisoner in Rangoon's Insein Prison. Pinheiro said he was "shocked" by the incident and expressed frustration with the situation of Burma's 1,200–1,600 political prisoners.[57]

In December 2005, the International Committee of the Red Cross (ICRC), suspended visits to Burma's prisons after the USDA insisted on sitting in on the meetings. The ICRC's protocol requires that such visits be independent and unsupervised.

The final blow to the international community's efforts to ease the repression in Burma came when in March 2006 the generals expelled a Swiss-based conflict-resolution outfit, the Center for Humanitarian Dialogue, which had run a low-profile political reconciliation program since August 2000. The move came shortly after Razali Ismail, a Malaysian diplomat, decided to abandon his post as the UN's special envoy to Burma because of the SPDC's refusal of his numerous requests to visit the country.[58]

However, there was some degree of optimism when UN undersecretary general for political affairs, Ibrahim Gambari, paid a three-day visit to Burma in mid-May 2006. He held talks with Suu Kyi—the first outsider to do so since Razali met her in 2004—and left with the impression that the Burmese authorities appeared to be preparing for her release. He thought the generals seemed willing to "open a new chapter in relations with the international community."[59] Gambari also met Than Shwe, who he said was "prepared to turn over a new page," and move forward towards some kind of national reconciliation.

A new page in Than Shwe's book, yes, but Suu Kyi's name was not on it. On May 27 (2+7=9), less than two weeks after Gambari's visit, her house arrest was extended for another year.[60]

CHAPTER 5

WHAT WENT WRONG?

The National League for Democracy (NLD) lost a golden opportunity in the days immediately after the May 1990 election. Against all expectations, the junta had shown some goodwill by holding a free and fair election, so the NLD thought it would then show some goodwill, too, by not pressing demands for Suu Kyi's release or for the convening of the newly elected parliament. The NLD did nothing, and that was a serious mistake. It gave the junta time to regroup and to strike back, which it did with its announcement on July 27, claiming that the MPs-elect were not actually MPs-elect, but that some of them—in the end about a quarter of those who had been elected—would become delegates to a constituent assembly, which they would have to share with hundreds of other handpicked, non-elected delegates.

It was only then that the NLD moved into action. On July 29, its MPs-elect met at the Gandhi Hall in downtown Rangoon and adopted a declaration urging the junta "to hold frank and sincere discussions with good faith and with the object of national reconciliation." It reminded the junta that its own election law stipulated that "the Pyithu Hluttaw [national assembly] shall be formed with the Hluttaw representatives who have been elected according to this law from the constituencies," and that "only the Pyithu Hluttaw represented by us has the responsibility to adopt the new constitution." In conclusion, the NLD MPs-elect called on the junta to "convene the Pyithu Hluttaw during September, 1990."[1]

But it was too late. The State Law and Order Restoration Council (SLORC) went after the pro-democracy movement with a vengeance. After crushing the monks' movement in Mandalay and arresting acting NLD leader Kyi Maung, it hit the NLD with a sledgehammer. More activists were arrested on trumped-up charges, and it become clear that the NLD would not under any circumstances be allowed to form a government. Gradually, the NLD crumbled under the pressure. Hundreds of activists resigned or became inactive. NLD offices were closed down all over the country.

Only a few stalwarts fled to the Thai border, where they linked up with Karen and other ethnic minority insurgents, as well as the students who had arrived at the frontier after the September 1988 massacre. Shortly after that first flight to the border, the National Democratic Front (NDF), an alliance of about a dozen ethnic rebel armies, had initiated a broader front, the Democratic Alliance of Burma (DAB), which included all the members of the NDF, minus the Karenni, who insisted on their "independent" status and on not being part of Burma, plus about ten smaller Burman dissident groups. Of these only the All-Burma Students' Democratic Front (ABSDF) and the mainly US-based Committee for Restoration of Democracy in Burma (CRDB) were of any significance. But the DAB had been by and large unable to affect the situation inside the country.

With the arrival of the MPs-elect and a few dozen NLD cadres from the towns, this was supposed to change. At a grand ceremony at the Manerplaw headquarters of the Karen rebels on December 18, 1990, six MPs-elect proclaimed the formation of the National Coalition Government of the Union of Burma (NCGUB). It was headed by Sein Win, a first cousin of Aung San Suu Kyi. His father, Aung San's elder brother Ba Win, had been gunned down together with the independence hero in the Secretariat building in Rangoon on July 19, 1947. But that was Sein Win's only political credential. He was a mathematician who had graduated from universities in Rangoon and Hamburg and later taught in Sri Lanka and Kenya. He made no impression on foreigners he met at Manerplaw or, more often, in Bangkok or Washington. It soon became obvious that no foreign country was going to recognize his jungle-based "cabinet"—and the desperate move to place him in leadership reflected the dire straits into which the once mighty NLD had fallen.

The NLD had been decapitated for the first time in July 1989, when Suu Kyi, Tin U, and all the other top leaders of the league had been incarcerated. A second-rung leadership headed by Kyi Maung had taken over. He was hardly of the same caliber as his arrested colleagues but had proved strong enough to carry the NLD through its election victory in May 1990.

Then, four months later—when he, too, was arrested—the NLD was decapitated a second time, and third-rung leaders took over. In the border areas were Sein Win and his colleagues, and in Rangoon, the NLD announced that its new official chairman was Aung Shwe, a former army officer who had served as ambassador to Australia in the early 1980s. It was not difficult for the SLORC to cow him, a meek, colorless figure, and the rest of the third-rung NLD leadership, into submission. By the end of 1990, Burma's pro-democracy movement was effectively crushed, or driven into the hills, or even into exile.

What the NLD should have done after its victory at the polls, "if they had been real Gandhians and understood what civil disobedience means," an Indian diplomat commented at the time, was to have taken advantage of the unprecedented openness that the SLORC had permitted during the election.[2] The election result must have come as a complete shock to the SLORC, which remained inactive for weeks after the astonishing election.

As soon as the outcome was clear, and it became evident that the NLD had won with a landslide, they should have called a press conference at their Rangoon headquarters. The international media, including foreign TV crews with their own satellite feeds, were in Burma at the time, and the press conference would have been telecast live all over the world. The NLD should then have claimed victory and announced that, because of the massive mandate the people had given them, they would now go and liberate their leader, Suu Kyi, from her house arrest. Loudspeaker cars should then have crisscrossed Rangoon, urging everyone to gather on University Avenue. A million people would have shown up, and they could easily have unhinged the gates to Suu Kyi's compound and carried her to Burma's television studios, where she could have addressed the people, appealed for calm, and urged the armed forces to be loyal to the new government.

Given the fact that the election result showed that even the rank and file of the army had voted for the NLD, it is unlikely that the soldiers in the streets would have tried to stop the masses of people. It would have been all over in a day. The SLORC could have been given amnesty, and, if they so wanted, been permitted to leave the country for Singapore, China, or any other country that would have been willing to accommodate them.

But that never happened. The NLD waited—and let its election victory slip out of its hands. The military will never allow a similar situation to happen again. It enforced its will on the people, and without a proper leadership to carry on the struggle, there was little the public could do but get on with their lives and forget about democracy.

Even in the border areas, the SLORC was having its way. Not only did it manage to neutralize more than twenty ethnic rebel armies through its generous cease-fire offers, but the remaining rebels also lost ground to the government's forces. In late January 1995, Manerplaw—the last bastion of resistance to the SLORC inside Burma—fell to the Burmese army. The Karen became an irregular guerrilla force without any permanent bases; the fighters of the ABSDF became refugees in Thailand, or were resettled in the United States, Australia, and Europe.

But the SLORC was well aware of its negative international reputation, and the need to do something about it. It had to appear legitimate in the eyes of the international community. Rather than change its ways, however, it began to hire lobbyists to persuade the outside world, and especially the Americans, the regime's fiercest critics, that the military government was not as bad as people thought. These efforts, however, turned out to be one public relations disaster after another.

In August 1991, the SLORC hired its first lobbyists—Van Kloberg & Associates in Washington, D.C. The contract that Burma's then ambassador to the United States, U Thaung, signed with Van Kloberg required the firm to "attract American business investment in Myanmar and facilitate business transactions," and to "counter the unrestrained negative representation of Myanmar and its administration."[3] It is unclear who introduced U Thaung to Edward Van Kloberg III, an infamous lobbyist who specialized in consulting for Third World despots and dictators, and hardly the person the Burmese generals needed to polish up their international image. Among his earlier clients were Samuel Doe of Liberia, Mobutu Sese Seko of Zaire, Iraq's Saddam Hussein, and erstwhile Rwandan president Juvenal Habyarimana.

Even those dictators turned out to be more trustworthy than Burma's generals. In the end, they did not pay their bills to Van Kloberg, and he called U Thaung "a little shit. . . . It was just ridiculous, I worked directly with him, I saw him constantly. . . . Wrote him daily, weekly, monthly reports. And then they stiffed me for about $5,000."[4]

Two years later, the junta hired another public relations agent to represent their interests in the United States. To the astonishment of many, this was Lester Wolff, a former US congressman who had advocated for human rights and alternative drug policies, including negotiations with the ethnic rebels who controlled the poppy fields. Now he began to use the drug issue to reach out to US policymakers. This was quite remarkable, as the cease-fire agreements that the junta had reached with the forces of the former Communist Party of Burma (CPB) and some other groups had enabled the latter to expand their drug production. According to the terms of the agreements, the cease-fire groups were unofficially permitted to engage in any kind of trade in exchange for not fighting the government's forces. As a result, Burma's production of opium and its derivative heroin skyrocketed, from 500–600 tons a year before the cease-fires, to more than 2,000 tons during the 1996–97 harvesting season. Satellite imagery showed that the area under poppy cultivation increased from 92,300 hectares in 1987, to 142,700 in 1989, and 154,000 in 1995, at the same time as cultivation techniques were improved, resulting in a higher yield per hectare.[5]

Both the United Nations International Drug Control Programme—now renamed the United Nations Office on Drugs and Crime—and the US Drug Enforcement Administration, DEA, were willing to play along with the junta, as its new allies in the border areas staged drug-burning shows and announced that they had initiated lavish "crop substitution schemes." In recent years, opium production has been somewhat reduced, but the traffickers have begun to manufacture methamphetamines and other synthetic drugs instead. Under the SLORC and its successor, the State Peace and Development Council (SPDC), narcotics have become one of Burma's few really lucrative export commodities, and drugs have kept flowing out of the country in all directions, to Thailand, China, India, and beyond.

At the same time, for $10,000 a month, Lester Wolff agreed to "help improve relations between our two peoples and our two governments . . . to the better understanding of the view and policies of the Union of Myanmar in the United States."[6]

Along with assorted American businessmen, several former congressmen and politicians went on all-expenses-paid "fact-finding" tours of Burma under the care and guidance of the Burmese military. The trips differed little from the well-orchestrated propaganda trips which, for instance, the Soviet Union organized for Western intellectuals in the 1930s. While thousands of political prisoners languished in jail, playwright George Bernard Shaw and others had praised Josef Stalin for "blessing the Soviet people with plenty."[7]

In a similar vein, the US "Honest Ballot Association" submitted a report on May 6, 1993, following a trip to Burma stating that

> Myanmar believes that it is being treated unfairly and is anxious to tell and show its side of the issue. . . . We also found a government that seems to be trying to make real economic and social progress while at the same time maintaining sufficient control to keep its many divergent ethnic and national forces from causing a complete disintegration.[8]

The delegation seemed deeply impressed by the "anti-drug activities" of the Burmese military, and on March 28, they "had the opportunity to meet with leaders of Myanmar's National Races." A list of these "leaders," however, revealed that all of them were former CPB commanders, now turned drug lords. The "Honest Ballot Association" concluded that Suu Kyi was a divisive force in Burmese politics and recommended a resumption of US assistance to Burma. The dossier presented by the delegation on its return also contained a letter from the DEA's Burma country attaché, Richard Horn, in which he listed "recent Government of Burma achievements in narcotics law enforcement" and praised the participants for coming to Burma to "acquire first-hand knowledge of the drug trafficking problem."

But there were few takers in Washington, and the "Honest Ballot Association" only discredited itself in the eyes of the American public and US officials. In June 1996, the US embassy in Rangoon released a detailed account of Burma's black economy in its yearly Foreign Economic Trends Report. It highlighted statistical discrepancies, or what economists call "errors and omissions," in the country's balance of payments. By comparing Rangoon's official trade figures with statistics from a variety of sources—including the United Nations Conference on Trade and Development, the International Monetary Fund, the Australian National University, and the Centre Française du Commerce Extérieur in Paris—the author of the report discovered $400 million in unexplained foreign financial inflows during 1995–96, up from $79 million the previous year.[9]

The economist explained that this was basically money that had come into the legal economy, and which was not reported by any of Burma's trading partners in official export-import statistics—in short, that it came from smuggling. In addition, Burma spent an estimated $200 million annually on foreign-currency-denominated defense expenditures that are not recorded in official reports. This, the economist argued, had to be added to the total amount of money in circulation that could not be explained in terms of official trade. Thus, the actual figure for money that could not be accounted for in fiscal 1995–96 was $600 million.

But why must hundreds of millions in proceeds from smuggling necessarily be drug money? The answer is that the only two other items that Burma produces that could generate such large sums of foreign exchange—jade and precious stones—are no longer smuggled to neighboring countries. The jade trade was previously in the hands of ethnic Kachin rebels who controlled the mines around Hpakan in Kachin State. But in 1993–94, the government took over the jade mines, and the trade has since then gone through official channels via Rangoon. The same applies to the gemstone mines in the northeast: mining rights in the region are subcontracted to private entrepreneurs by the military-controlled Myanmar Economic Holdings, which collects duties on the trade.

A number of private companies have also benefited, directly or indirectly, from the new arrangements in the border areas. In 1992, Lo Hsing-han—a drug lord from the Kokang area in northeastern Shan State, who was sentenced to death in 1976, but pardoned and released from jail under a general amnesty in 1980—and his family set up the company Asia World, which a diplomatic report from Rangoon described as "Burma's fastest growing and most diversified conglomerate."

The company became involved in import-export business, bus transport, housing and hotel construction, a supermarket chain, Rangoon's port development, and the upgrading of the highway between Mandalay and Muse on the Chinese border. Its Memorandum of Association under the Myanmar Companies Act identifies Lo Hsing-han and his son Htun Myint Naing (Steven Law), as major shareholders. Other partners include known drug traffickers from Kokang. In 1996, Steven Law was refused a visa to the US on suspicion of involvement in narcotics trafficking. But Asia World remains the main contractor besides Htoo Trading that is involved in the construction of the new capital at Naypyidaw.

It is clear to most observers that drug money was fuelling the Burmese economy—and that a new, different image could not be bought like a commodity. But that did not deter the Burmese generals from hiring yet another lobbyist in 1997. Using a Burmese real estate developer, Zay Ka Bar, as a front, they contacted Jackson Bain, a former television network White House correspondent turned public relations consultant. They agreed to pay Bain $250,000 annually to show the media a kinder, gentler Burma. Myanmar Resources Development, Ltd., another front company for the junta, also hired Jefferson Waterman International for the same purpose, paying $400,000 a year and some $100,000 in expenses to arrange contacts between the authorities in Rangoon and officials from the US administration and to "educate the media" about the situation in Burma.[10]

Not only were those public relations drives costly, but the results were also unconvincing. Jefferson Waterman arranged press trips to Burma, but the resultant reporting was mostly highly critical of the Burmese military regime.[11] The only lasting result of Jefferson Waterman's PR drive was that the firm in November 1997 managed to persuade the SLORC to change its name to the less sinister-sounding SPDC.

But the junta did not give up so easily. In April 2002, it hired yet another PR firm to help improve its international image. This time DCI Associates, a firm headed by Thomas J. Synhorst, a well-known Republican lobbyist with close connections to President George W. Bush and the tobacco industry, was paid $340,000 for eight months of work, most of which hinged on persuading the US to certify Burma as compliant with drug control standards. That effort failed as well, however, and provoked a strong statement from Senator Mitch McConnell, a Republican from Kentucky. He referred to a common practice in the Burmese army of giving its young soldiers methamphetamines and alcohol prior to combat. "American State Department officials should not be deluded into believing that Burma has become a partner in the war against drugs.... Countries that force drugged children into deadly combat should not be considered allies by the United States in any war."[12]

On the other hand, the NLD—and Suu Kyi when she was free and had a chance to address her people and the outside world—has not formulated a comprehensive drug policy either, or a blueprint for a solution to Burma's perennial ethnic crisis.

These two intertwined issues must be seen as the most important of Burma's many problems that have to be solved if the country is going to develop into a modern state. Not even the NCGUB, which was based together with ethnic minority groups in the border areas and thus had access to relevant information on the drug issue, has tried to counter the official propaganda about the phony "war on drugs." The only accounts of the junta's involvement with the drug traffickers have been published by a Shan interest group, the Shan Herald Agency for News (SHAN). Its April 2005 report, "Show Business: Rangoon's 'War on Drugs' in Shan State," and a subsequent report in 2006, "Hand in Glove: The Burma Army and the Drug Trade in Shan State," lay out in great detail the SPDC's complicity in the drug trade and conclude that "the regime's principal focus is controlling the opposition, not the welfare of the people, and therefore definitely not on drugs." On the contrary, the drug trade brings in millions to the Burmese economy at a time when most other sectors have failed to generate significant profits.

Still, the United Nations Office on Drugs and Crime continues to praise the junta's "drug control measures," and Burma's efforts to gain support from other foreign parties have not been totally fruitless. Before the August 1988 uprising, Burma was a fool's paradise where few bothered to find out the bitter realities of the repression in the country. When Amnesty International in May of that year released a detailed report on human rights abuses in the country, titled "Burma: Extrajudicial Executions and Torture of Members of Ethnic Minorities," most foreign diplomats in Rangoon dismissed it as "exaggerated." The UN's handsomely paid bureaucrats in the then Burmese capital did not even react.

The isolation of the foreigners in Burma was part of the tragedy. Even contacts between government officials and foreign diplomats were kept at an absolute minimum. Burton Levin, then US ambassador to Burma, commented in an extraordinarily frank speech at the Asia Society in New York on November 29, 1988,

> We had no meaningful contact with any element of the Burmese government. They had a designated group of foreign ministry types who would come to our dinners and talk about golf and tennis, the weather and what fruits were in season. . . . During my first three months in Burma, my backhand improved immensely, and I even took up the game of golf, which I had thought was just a waste of time. But I had time to waste.[13]

In August and September 1988, however, the traditional image of Burma collapsed like the fragile house of cards it had always been. Diplomats were outraged and felt almost personally betrayed by the government's officials and the army officers they had befriended—those who now sent their troops to gun down unarmed demonstrators, sometimes in full view of the embassies in central Rangoon.

But as the years went by, that old fool's paradise was restored. Attracting foreign investment was one way of gaining legitimacy and the support of foreign businessmen who were eager to get into this "new market" when the Burmese Way to Socialism was abandoned in late 1988. Despite some initial hesitation, by 1990 hundreds of foreign companies were doing business in Burma.

Most of them did not make much money, however, as the military's erratic economic policies made it almost impossible to run a normal business in the country. The joke was that for a foreign businessman to become a millionaire in Burma, it was best to arrive as a billionaire. But many foreign businessmen tended to blame Suu Kyi and her appeals for sanctions for their misfortunes rather than the SPDC's inept, so-called economic reform program.

Rangoon-based diplomats and UN officials were also targets of the junta's charm offensive, which was far more successful in the country than internationally. Soon some of them became, in effect, Burma's ambassadors to their own countries instead of vice versa, putting forth irrelevant arguments like "It's just as bad in Laos," or "What freedom is there in Singapore?" or "Child labor? It's worse in India, which is a democracy."[14]

For diplomats, UN officials, and foreign businessmen, Rangoon has become a comparatively comfortable place to live. It is green, leafy, and pleasant, and no one talks openly any longer about the brutal repression in 1988, or the more than a thousand political prisoners who are still incarcerated in the country's many prisons and labor camps. Because of the lack of transparency and accountability, and the absence of any investigative and critical media, Burma provides plenty of opportunities for corruption and private business deals, such as the smuggling of antiques in diplomatic and UN bags, and the sale of duty free goods on the black market.

On Fridays, the expatriates meet for drinks in the venerable—and now reverentially renovated—Strand Hotel by the Rangoon River waterfront, or they sip beer and cocktails at the chic Ginki Kids near the Shwegondaing Junction, not far from the NLD's headquarters. Most of the expatriates in Rangoon cannot be bothered with the country's pro-democracy movement. It is bad for business.

Some of them have also become open propagandists for the regime, not just exchanging gossip in bars in Rangoon. One of them is Michael

Dobbs-Higginson, a white Zimbabwean. A former chairman of Merrill Lynch Asia Pacific, he now spends most of his time in Hong Kong. But, in the 1990s, he was active in Burma and later wrote a book about the Asia-Pacific region, *Asia-Pacific: Its Role in the New World Disorder,* which purports to provide "a fascinating and unique insight into a much-misunderstood region . . . by a man with a formidable thirty-year track record in the region." Its Burma chapter stands out as amazingly naive and ill-informed. The 1988 uprising is described in these terms:

> As the country was literally in a state of anarchy, the *Tatmadaw* (armed forces) formed the State Law and Order Restoration Council (SLORC) on September 18, 1988 to ensure law and order, safe transportation and communication, adequate food, housing and other essential public needs and the preparation for holding of multi-party, democratic elections—all in the interest of both the state and the people.[15]

Suu Kyi, Dobbs-Higginson argued, could not be trusted.

> Sensationalist cries that Daw Aung San Suu Kyi is another Nelson Mandela or Benazir Bhutto must be tempered with reason. Quite clearly she is a remarkable woman and her six-year refusal to be released from house arrest on the proviso that she left Myanmar is admirable. However, it must be noted that, after some twenty-eight years abroad, she only returned to Myanmar in July 1988 to help her terminally ill mother. Suu Kyi's home-coming coincided with the then countrywide anarchy and she was catapulted onto the public stage by virtue of being General Aung San's daughter and her own innate decency. Despite this, objectively it must be recognised that she had no leadership experience, was only in her forties, was very idealistic, was approached by a wide range of variously inexperienced and experienced self-interest groups, and was supported *a la* Tiananmen Square, by student activists. Her English husband, Michael Aris, an academic, took upon himself the rather Don Quixote-like role of roving, international ambassador for the Burmese democratic movement. To say the least, the pair made a very inexperienced, and thus potentially dangerous, combination.[16]

Apart from getting some of his facts wrong—Syu Kyi returned to Burma in April, not July 1988—Dobbs-Higginson had clearly been taken in by the charm of the Burmese generals, believing everything he was told. "In short, having now made many visits to Myanmar over the last two years to discover for myself what is happening, I confess freely that I was wrong in my initial international-media led, negative judgement. Many others too could be wrong."[17]

So it was the international media's fault that thousands of people have died in the hands of the junta, and that even more are being incarcerated, tortured, or forced to become refugees in Burma's neighboring countries. His only valid point may be Suu Kyi's inexperience, and indeed the inexperience of her movement, which led to the mistakes the NLD made after the May 1990 election and the loss of the only opportunity the party had to assume power.

Now that Suu Kyi is in her sixties, not in her forties, she certainly has more leadership qualities than, for instance, Than Shwe. Her main problem is the lack of competent people around her; the NLD is not the African National Congress, which had many able leaders and could function as a mass movement even though Nelson Mandela was in prison. Apart from Suu Kyi herself, there is nobody left in the NLD who is strong enough to carry the movement forward.

On the other hand, the world—and even the Burmese themselves—do not know enough about her actual capacities. Although she has been a democracy icon for nearly two decades, her active political life has been confined to the period from August 1988 to July 1989—or not even a year—followed by five highly restricted years of semi-freedom from 1995 to 2000, then another year of even more limited political activity from May 2002 to May 2003. She has spent the rest of her time, or more than a decade, under house arrest.

It is often said of her famous and deeply revered father that he died a hero because he died young. He was only thirty-two when he was gunned down in Rangoon, and had not had much time to commit any serious mistakes—apart from siding with the Japanese during the war, and meandering between communism and fascism before eventually deciding that he wanted to be a democrat. There was also a murder charge against Aung San. When he and his comrades marched into Burma, Aung San had personally killed a village headman who was accused of pro-British activities and corruption. When the war was over, some British officers wanted to have Aung San arrested and tried for the crime but in the end it was decided that such a move could spark a rebellion against the colonial power and hamper the independence process, so the case was dropped.[18]

Aung San signed the Panglong Agreement with some ethnic leaders, but it is doubtful that he would have been able to prevent the country from plunging into civil war after independence. How would he have handled the Karen insurgency, which would have broken out anyway, the Karen not being party to the Panglong Agreement? How would he have handled the communist insurgency? Burma's role in the region? Relations with Britain, the United States, China, and Japan? No one knows, because he did not live to become the first leader of an independent Burma. Similarly, no one knows how Suu Kyi would handle similar problems today, because she has never had a chance to lead the country, and she has been cut off from the outside world for years with only brief stints of freedom.

Somewhat alarmingly, she has indeed said nothing, or very little, about the sufferings of the people in the minority areas, where the military continues to terrorize civilians simply because they live in a part of the country where insurgents are active. The global humanitarian agency Church World Service estimated in September 2006 that the military has driven one million ethnic civilians from their homes, of whom more than half are internally displaced inside the country.[19]

On the other hand, the pro-democracy exiles, who are based mainly in Thailand but also in India, Bangladesh, and China and have raised these issues, have at the same time been cut off from the main political scene inside the country. Far from acting as a government in exile, the NCGUB has become just another group among others in the increasingly factionalized pro-democracy movement abroad. For most of the Thailand-based groups, survival—not political change in Burma—has become the overriding priority. They advocate "dialogue" and "national reconciliation"—catchwords that are popular with international donor but of little or no relevance to developments inside Burma, where the military talks to no one except themselves.

Attempts to forge workable alliances to coordinate the struggle have failed, mainly because the individual groups have to compete for donor money. And money has kept coming from the National Endowment for Democracy and George Soros's Open Society Institute in the US, the Norwegian government, Danish and Swedish aid organizations, church groups all over the world, and private donors.

Not surprisingly, a rift has emerged between the exiles and the activists who are still in the country. While the exiles in Thailand are active publishing a flurry of magazines and journals and holding endless meetings and workshops on subjects such as "democracy and the media," "women in development," and "capacity building," they have become a world to themselves where they preach to the converted. And despite occasional raids by the Thai police, they can, by and large, work freely without fear of being arrested or deported.

Inside the country, however, there is an entirely different reality. "We recognize that opponents of the regime living in exile are doing a good job and are part of the struggle for democracy. But we have made the decision to stay here and lead the struggle from the front.... Call us the generation of 1988. We are the front line in the struggle for democracy," a Burmese man in his thirties told a foreign reporter in September 2005.[20]

Those who were young student activists in 1988 are now in their late thirties or early forties, and they meet regularly in teashops in Rangoon to discuss politics. Most of them have spent years in jail, "plucked from their families, from their studies," to quote the foreign reporter. "At last free, they still live in a kind of captivity—watched by the regime's agents, unable to find jobs in any official capacity, locked out of the universities and colleges which once offered them the promise of relatively rewarding academic careers."[21]

The most prominent among the so-called "'88 Generation" is Min Ko Naing, the student leader who was arrested in March 1989—and released only in November 2005, having spent nearly sixteen years in solitary confinement. In 1988, he was a twenty-six-year old zoology student addressing crowds of tens of thousands in Rangoon; when he was released, he was forty-two, and his years in prison had left their marks on his face and body. In 2005, he looked old and haggard, but his fighting spirit had not been quelled. "The people of Burma must have the courage to say no to injustice and yes to the truth," he said at a meeting of the newly formed '88 Generation Students' Group in Rangoon in August 2006. "They must also work to correct their own wrongdoing that hurts society."[22]

Many countries in Asia have certain "generations" that fought for democracy, and sacrificed much of their lives for it. In South Korea, the term "386 generation" was coined in the 1990s to describe those who were born in the 1960s, attended university, and fought for democracy in the 1980s. Now in their forties, many of them are university lecturers, lawyers, newspaper columnists, or even ministers in the government. They are the new elite, who are admired by the public at large because of their past sacrifices.

In Thailand, people speak of the "1970s generation": men and women who took to the streets in October 1973 and managed to force that country's then military government, led by Field Marshal Thanom Kittikachorn, into exile. Three years later, Thanom and some of his associates returned to Thailand, which caused a new wave of student-led protests. The protests, however, were crushed by the military, and thousands of students, teachers, and labor activists took to the jungle where they joined the insurgent Communist Party of Thailand (CPT). But they were hardly communists, and before long they fell out with the diehard CPT leadership. Following a general amnesty in 1980, almost all of them returned to Bangkok and other cities, where they, too, became prominent political and literary figures. To have been with the CPT in the jungle in the 1970s bears no stigma; on the contrary, they are respected because they endured hardships and continued to fight for what they believed in.

Burma now has its '88 generation, and it is coming of age—and they are not only meeting in teashops. Many have become journalists and writers. Burma has five daily newspapers that are published by the government, but—contrary to what is generally assumed in the outside world—the majority of the country's journals and magazines are privately owned. Publishing licenses are more easily obtained by those with strong connections to the government, however.

Burma today has nearly four hundred newspapers, journals, and magazines, and the number is growing steadily. In November 2005 the government issued fifteen new publishing licenses. These publications may operate under some of the most restrictive laws and regulations in the world, but they are nevertheless becoming bolder and more outspoken in their reporting. In fact, the media in Burma has become one of the few dynamic sectors in a society that remains mostly stagnant.

Local journalists and editors often state that their main motivation for getting into the profession is "public service" and a desire "to do something for the country."[23] Many are interested in politics and development, and find that journalism—despite all the constraints placed upon them—is one of the few professions that allows them to play a role in current events in a constructive fashion. Many took part in the 1988 uprising and remain faithful to their democratic ideals.

If any political or social force is going to play an important role in Burma's future and carry the country's unfinished renaissance forward, it is not the increasingly geriatric NLD, but men and women of this new '88 generation. The government soon realized their political potential and reacted in its own inimitable way. On September 27, 2006, police arrested Min Ko Naing along with two other former political prisoners, Ko Ko Gyi and Ko Htay Kywe. Each had spent fifteen years in the Burmese military's notorious prisons, but they had not given up hope for a better future for Burma.

Their arrest turned out to be counterproductive, because the '88 Generation is a generation, not a political party. On October 2, their comrades who had not been jailed started an unprecedented nationwide signature campaign. People put their names under demands for freedom for Burma's political prisoners, and they could also in a few words express their grievances and desires. When the campaign ended on October 23, more than half a million signatures had been collected all over the country. The results were sent to the UN headquarters in New York.

At the same time, the '88 Generation urged citizens across the country to participate in a "Multiple Religious Prayer" to be held in Buddhist and Hindu temples, Christian churches, and Muslim mosques.[24] People flocked to the holy sites, dressed in white, the symbol of the sacrifices of Burma's many martyrs. The government was probably taken aback by this massive, but entirely peaceful, expression of dissent. A few more people were arrested, but then there were no more repressive measures. The generals were busy building their new royal capital, Naypyidaw.

The '88 Generation now is a force to be reckoned with, although it has no proper leadership or organization. They, in fact, see Suu Kyi as their leader. "She is the one person that can bring about reconciliation and lead us into a new, democratic future," one of the activists told a foreign reporter who interviewed them in September 2005.[25]

Then, in 2007, unrest spread beyond the circle of veterans of the 1988 uprising as the people of Burma once again took to the streets to vent their frustrations with the country's military government. The protests were sparked by a government decision on August 15 to increase the price of fuel. Both petrol and diesel doubled in price, while the cost of compressed gas—used to power buses—increased five-fold. Four days later, about 400 people, mostly housewives, marched through the old capital, Rangoon. The authorities reacted swiftly, arresting more than 1,009 activists, among them Min Ko Naing, who went back to jail after a brief spell of freedom.

But that did not stop the protests. The monks started participating and, on September 5 in the central town of Pakokku, the troops and police used force to break up a peaceful rally. Several monks were beaten badly, and the next day the monks captured about twenty government officials and locked them up in a monastery. They were released shortly afterwards, but the monks demanded an apology from the authorities for the beatings.

When no apology was forthcoming, the monks began to protest in much greater numbers. Tens of thousands marched through the streets of Rangoon and the country's second city, Mandalay. Laypeople soon joined in, and in Rangoon up to 100,000 took part in the demonstrations, which turned into the most massive popular manifestation against the regime since the 1988 uprising. The movement took a very definite political turn when, on September 22, monks and laypeople marched past the barricades blocking the road leading up to Suu Kyi's home, where she was then still under house arrest. She emerged briefly through the gates of her compound, in tears at the sight of the monks, who chanted from the Buddhist scriptures and blessed her.

The next day, the barricades were reinforced, most probably because the decision to let the people through had been taken by the local police chief in Rangoon—much to the displeasure of the country's ruling military junta. Then, the crackdown began. Troops were brought in from the country's border areas, where a multitude of ethnic insurgents are active, and they raided monasteries, manhandled monks, and stole gold, TV sets, and other items from their living quarters. In the streets, troops supported by riot police charged the demonstrations, first shooting in the air, then into the crowds. Scores were killed and hundreds arrested.

The violence against what had been entirely peaceful demonstrations led by Buddhist monks drove the people off the streets. But it deepened the hatred most ordinary Burmese harbor against their repressive government, and it caused an international outcry. State leaders, politicians, and advocacy groups all over the world condemned Burma's hard-line generals, but nothing seemed to move them. According to their version, they added insult to injury by claiming that they had acted "softly" and "with care."

The international condemnation of the September 2007 carnage in Rangoon soon fizzled out. The ruling military knew how to play their cards, and the chance came in the first week of May 2008, when Cyclone Nargis devastated the Irrawaddy delta, Burma's rice bowl and home to millions of farmers. At least 130,000 people were killed and 2.4 million made homeless or affected in other ways. It was the worst natural disaster in Asia since the December 2004 tsunami. More than 40 percent of those affected were children—in a region where young people already suffered from malnutrition. Drinking water was in short supply, as most sources had been contaminated by decomposing corpses. Entire villages were wiped out with hardly a building left standing, except for the Buddhist temples, usually built from stronger material than ordinary, wooden houses. Crops were destroyed by saltwater seeping into the fields, which may have a devastating long-term impact on the country's food supply.

The world wanted to rush to assist the victims, but the country's military government responded by retreating into its shell and turning down offers of help. The US amphibious assault ship USS *Essex* was moored off Burma's southern coast, while the French naval ship *Le Mistral* waited in the same waters. Tens of thousands of gallons of drinking water, ambulances, heavy trucks, and medical teams could have reached Burma within an hour by helicopter and landing craft from the USS *Essex*. *Le Mistral* carried a cargo of 1,000 tons of food, enough to feed at least 100,000 people for two weeks, as well as thousands of shelters for the homeless.

Having waited for weeks, they eventually had to leave when the Burmese government refused to let them bring their goods ashore. The Burmese people were told to fend for themselves, and private citizens who had organized relief efforts were arrested. One of them was the famous comedian Zargarnar, who together with other artists, entertainers, and Buddhist monks, had collected tons of food, water, medicines, and other supplies and sent them down to the Irrawaddy delta. Zargarnar was a well-known pro-democracy activist who had entertained the demonstrators during the August–September 1988 uprising with biting satires. In the midst of all the carnage and misery following the August massacres, he had made people laugh and infuriated the military, as he made fun of them. He was arrested several times in the 1980s and 1990s, and on June 4, 2008, he was rearrested for speaking to foreign media about the situation of millions of people left homeless after the cyclone and was sentenced to fifty-nine years in prison.

Meanwhile, the official newspaper, *The New Light of Myanmar*, assured its readers that hunger could not be a problem, since farmers can gather edible water plants or "go out with lamps at night and catch plump frogs." And to show that the government was on top of the situation, planning minister Soe Tha stated in a truly Orwellian manner that "665,271 ducks, 56,163 cows, and 1,614,502 chickens have been lost in the storm—along with 35,051 acres of fish ponds and 22,200 metric tons of beef."[26]

Only after severe pressure from the international community, including the United Nations and Burma's neighbors and fellow members in the Association of Southeast Asian Nations (ASEAN), did the regime allow some aid to reach the victims. But all efforts were strictly supervised by the country's military authorities, and the movements of aid workers were severely restricted.

The world was flabbergasted. How could any regime do this to its own people? It was a natural disaster with no one to blame, and the aid that was offered came with no strings attached. But from the junta's perspective, refusing aid made some obscene sense. If foreign troops—which should have overseen the distribution of supplies—had entered Burma, their presence could have emboldened the country's citizens to launch yet another uprising against the regime. Ordinary Burmese were already angered because of a bloody crackdown on pro-democracy demonstrations led by Buddhist monks the year before. If anti-government activists thought they could count on foreign protection—even if the foreign troops were in Burma on a purely humanitarian mission—they could have taken to the streets again. Hence, troops from foreign countries that have criticized the regime and expressed support for Burma's pro-democracy movement had to be kept out at all cost, no matter how much food and medicine they could have supplied.

Gradually the international community was allowed in to distribute aid to the victims of Cyclone Nargis. It was a precarious arrangement, and no one wanted to upset things by "embarrassing" the regime by reminding it of how callous it had been during the first weeks of the disaster—or how it had brutally crushed the monks' movement of 2007. Soon, foreign aid agencies began praising the government for its unprecedented "openness."

And few critical voices were heard during or after a highly unusual step that the military authorities took just as millions of people in southern Burma's coastal areas were reeling from the devastation of Cyclone Nargis. On May 10, 2008, a referendum was held on a new constitution, which would secure a leading role for the military in governing the country. The referendum was postponed only in the forty-seven worst-hit townships in Irrawaddy and Rangoon Divisions—and, if official figures are to be believed, 92.4 percent of voters approved the charter, with a 99 percent turnout. Two weeks later, on May 24, voters in Rangoon and the

Irrawaddy delta affirmed the constitution by an even more resounding 92.93 percent, the state-run *New Light of Myanmar* newspaper reported.

Only groups such as Human Rights Watch reported that, "The government-controlled media offers only crude propaganda in favor of a 'Yes' vote, and talks of criminal penalties for those who oppose the referendum, creating a climate of fear. There has been no critical public discussion of the constitution's contents; most people have not even seen the document. The generals are sending a clear message that their handcrafted constitution will continue the military rule that has persisted for more than four decades."[27]

To ensure the continuation of that military rule, the SPDC went ahead and eventually held its promised election on November 7, 2010. But the election aroused more interest internationally—Burma pundits all over the world began pondering on what it all meant for the country's "democratization process"—than among the Burmese public. There was little or no enthusiasm among a people who time and again had been cheated by their military rulers. In an interview with the *Irrawaddy*, NLD veteran Tin U said, "People seem lacking in enthusiasm over the vote. We are not seeing the kind of activeness of 1990. Many of those who are running [for election] have never breathed a word about democracy in their lives. So I was surprised when I read their campaign pamphlets. This election is the one that gets least public attention in our country's history, I would say."[28] The NLD had decided not to take part in the election, and, therefore, in May 2010, had been officially dissolved. But it continued to be a force to be reckoned with, and members of the former party continued to meet despite the dissolution.

Weeks before the election, sources inside Burma were reporting that the military wanted to make the election credible by producing official results that showed 70 percent voter turnout with 80 percent support for its own party, the Union Solidarity and Development Party (USDP), which was the old Union Solidarity and Development Association in new draping. And that was exactly the announced outcome after the November 7 election.

Some NLD members had disagreed with the decision to boycott the election and broke away to form the National Democratic Force (NDF).

Led by Dr. Than Nyein, who in 1990 had been elected from Kyauttan township in Rangoon and was also a former political prisoner, it did its best to take advantage of the tiny opening for political activities that the election, after all, provided. The outcome was perhaps predictable, though. In constituencies in Rangoon and elsewhere, where it seemed that the NDF was heading for victory, boxes of "advanced votes" were dumped, overturning the result in favor of the USDP. In some constituencies where the USDP was doing badly, the doors were simply closed when the votes were going to be counted. In the end, the NDF got altogether only sixteen of the 608 seats in the new assemblies, the Upper House, or Nationalities' Assembly (where 168 are elected and 56 reserved for the military), and the 440-seat Lower House, or People's Assembly (330 elected, and 110 for the military).

Another "third force" that fared badly because of electoral fraud or other reasons were the so-called "Three Princesses," daughters of leaders from Burma's democratic, pre-1962 era: U Nu's daughter Mya Than Than Nu, who had returned from exile in India; Nayee Ba Swe, whose father was briefly prime minister in 1956; and Cho Cho Kyaw Nyein, the daughter of Kyaw Nyein, deputy prime minister under U Nu. None of them was elected.[29]

It was clear that the new constitution, which had been adopted during the immediate aftermath of Cyclone Nargis, was specially designed to bar Suu Kyi from politics. Article 121 in effect bars her from holding any political office because of her marriage to a foreigner, the fact that her two sons are "citizens of a foreign country," and because she has, as the article says, "been convicted . . . for having committed an offence." The military, on the other hand, was given a quarter of all seats in the bicameral legislature. Article 396 of the new constitution also ensures that MPs-elect can be dismissed for "misbehavior" by the Union Election Commission, which will remain indirectly controlled by the military. And, if the "democratic" situation gets really out of hand, Article 413 gives the president the right to hand over executive powers to the commander-in-chief of the armed forces.[30] There is no doubt that the November 7 election was designed to institutionalize the present order, not to change it.

With power now firmly in their hands even constitutionally, the military went ahead and released Suu Kyi from house arrest on November 13. It was clear, though, that they were not interested in any dialogue with her, or with anybody else from the opposition. Suu Kyi's son Kim paid an emotional visit to Rangoon shortly after her release—it was the fist time in ten years that he had seen his mother—but local, privately owned magazines and journals were warned not to cover the event, or anything about her and her activities.[31]

Internationally, however, Suu Kyi's release diverted all international attention away from the fraudulent election. Younger Western diplomats, who had no memory of what it was like when Suu Kyi had toured the country during her brief spells of freedom in the 1980s, 1990s, and early 2000s, had until then dismissed her as irrelevant. They believed she had been gone from the scene for too long, that young people did not even know her, and that a viable third force had emerged to bridge the gap between the ruling military and the pro-democracy movement. Foreigners in Rangoon were astounded to see the size of the enthusiastic crowds that gathered to see her—and that many of them were young people, born after the 1988 uprising. The November 7 election and the scenes in Rangoon after Suu Kyi's release showed, therefore, that the so-called "third force" was just a figment of the imagination of outsiders eager to see an end to the political impasse in Burma.

In a similar misjudgment by the international community, a tiny group of intellectuals and social workers calling themselves "Myanmar Egress" had for several years attracted the attention of diplomats and foreign donors. The group is led by Dr. Nay Win Maung, a local media mogul, and Khin Zaw Win, an erstwhile UN employee and former political prisoner. According to its website, it was "set up in 2006 by a group of Myanmar nationalists committed to state building through positive change in a progressive yet constructive collaboration and working relationship with the government and all interest groups, both local and foreign"—reasonable-sounding objectives. It became a partner of groups such as Germany's Friedrich Ebert Stiftung, and many Western diplomats praised it as an excellent example of how a "compromise" could be reached in a badly divided country.[32] In September 2010, Khin Zaw

Win toured Europe in an attempt to persuade people that the upcoming election would provide "an opening for democracy."[33] These were words and promises Myanmar Egress had to regret when the election was over. David Mathieson, Burma researcher for Human Rights Watch, wrote on the website *Open Democracy* on November 24,

> Nay Win Maung, a prominent "third force" intellectual, magazine editor, and leader of an influential NGO (Myanmar Egress), was a notable proponent of the elections. He campaigned openly for people to participate; lobbied scores of western diplomats on how the elections promised change; and predicted a strong showing for the opposition, and the NUP (formerly the BSPP). On November 10, three days after the elections, he wrote—under his pseudonym "Aung Htut"—a short and contrite piece ("Those Who Climb the Slippery Pole") in his Burmese-language magazine *The Voice*: "We climbed a slippery pole, knowing it's slippery. I don't think we were wrong. I thought just by climbing it the first time, we would go rather far. That opinion was wrong. I am ready to take any blame for that. . . . I am not reluctant to apologise to the readers for giving them hope, and therefore, I would sincerely like to apologise to the readers."[34]

It was clear that there was no viable "third force" at all, no real middle ground between the ruling military and the population at large. Myanmar Egress may be the favorite of many outsiders, but most Burmese have probably never heard of it, and those who have could not care less about Nay Win Maung and his associates. After his frank admission in *The Voice* that he had been wrong and misjudged the situation in Burma, he may have difficulty convincing even the international community that his assessments remain sound and credible.

The truth that many are unwilling to accept is that Burma remains as bitterly divided as ever. But now that Suu Kyi once again has been released from house arrest she would like to prove that she is a social and political modernizer, not just a "spiritual person" who takes advice from nonagenarian monks. Suu Kyi's strength is her ability to rally people around her and make them listen to her message. Her weakness is her quest for a "revolution of the spirit," which smacks of obscurantism and sheer metaphysics.[35] Her son Alexander touched on the concept of a "revolution of the spirit" in his speech accepting the Nobel Peace Prize in Oslo in December 1991, and Suu Kyi herself has said that "a people who would build a nation in which strong democratic institutions are firmly established as a guarantee against state-induced power must first learn to liberate their own minds from apathy and fear."[36]

In other words, the struggle for democracy "is a struggle to cleanse one's own mind," to quote Dutch Burma scholar Gustaaf Houtman. Suu Kyi's father, Aung San, on the other hand, "looked forward and attempted to give leadership a more modern intellectual framework."[37] There is no doubt that Suu Kyi was deeply devoted to her country and its people even before she became a public figure in August 1988—which her letters to Michael Aris in the early 1970s clearly demonstrated—and that she remains so, despite years of house arrest and isolation. But it is to be doubted whether her practical father, whose unfinished work she has said she wants to continue, would have approved of her religious speculations, and outright prevarications when asked about her political plans and visions.

For the time being, however, there is precious little Suu Kyi can do during her occasional meetings with UN officials other than appeal to the international community to put pressure on the military to be less repressive, though that has not helped much either. The other approach, the policy of "constructive engagement" pursued by Burma's partners in ASEAN, has proven equally fruitless. Burma was admitted into ASEAN in July 1997, but has snubbed its partners by going back on promises of political reforms, and in the process has become a burden for the bloc and an obstacle in its relations with the United States and the European Union.

Change would have to come from within the only institution that really matters in the country—its armed forces. Min Zaw Oo, a Burmese researcher, has analyzed various possible scenarios that could lead to state failure in Burma, and, therefore, political change by voluntary means, or a UN intervention that would lead to such change.[38] According to the first scenario, socioeconomic erosions could lead to another uprising, similar to that of 1988. "If there is another uprising in Burma, the most pivotal change will depend on how the military responds to the crisis." A popular uprising could divide the armed forces, but that could also lead to Burma's breaking up into different sectors controlled by different factions of the army or, in plain speak, civil war.

The second of Min Zaw Oo's scenarios is no uprising but infighting within the armed forces. The purge of Khin Nyunt and his intelligence faction in 2004 showed that there are serious divisions even within the military establishment. Khin Nyunt's fall from grace did not lead to serious infighting, but rivalry between Than Shwe and his deputy, Gen. Maung Aye, could well be such a catalyst for change. It would most certainly be bloody, and could also lead to civil war. In May 2005, a series of near-simultaneous explosions rocked shopping centers and supermarkets in Rangoon, wounding more than a dozen people. The authorities were quick to blame the blasts on "Thai-based terrorists," but these would hardly have the means to infiltrate the then capital. More likely, it could have been the work of disgruntled, former military intelligence officers who had been purged along with Khin Nyunt, or the junta itself, which needed an excuse to crack down on real or imaginary opponents to its rule.[39] Despite rigid military rule and control, Burma is far from a stable country. Chaos and internecine strife could easily break out at any time.

The third scenario is "the emergence of a reformist faction in the military that decides to cooperate with the civilian opposition to foster a political transition while the other significant forces resist any change in the status quo." But, as Min Zaw Oo also points out, the civilian opposition does not have adequate capacity to fill the power vacuum that such a split in the military would produce, and to form by itself a new government. Further, any state failure in Burma would have regional repercussions, as its neighbors would be affected by an even bigger flow of refugees, drugs, and weapons than is the case today.

State failure could also encourage the insurgents who now have ceasefire agreements with the government to go their own ways, and perhaps even declare independence from Naypyidaw. A Yugoslavia-style scenario is not unthinkable, and would also have disastrous consequences for the region. Politicians and statesmen in the region would rather see Suu Kyi focus on these problems than a "revolution of the spirit," thus mixing politics with Buddhist practices and concepts such as *vipassana* and *metta*.

Naturally, there was not much Suu Kyi could do as long as she was under house arrest and isolated from her people and the rest of the world. On the other hand, she did not take much advantage of the May 2006 visit by the UN undersecretary-general for political affairs, Ibrahim Gambari. She only called for more visits by UN dignitaries, and repeated the need for a dialogue. Many of her supporters were disappointed that she did not suggest anything concrete, or at the very least outline a plan of action for that dialogue to materialize.

Suu Kyi may be a heroine in the West and for social and political activists across Asia, but *realpolitik* dominates the thinking of the rulers of Burma's immediate neighbors. After the 1988 uprising, India almost openly supported the pro-democracy movement, partly because of then prime minister Rajiv Gandhi's old friendship with Suu Kyi. But as the influence of India's traditional rivals, China and Pakistan, grew in Burma—and it was becoming obvious that the pro-democracy movement was not going to assume power any time soon—New Delhi began to improve ties with the junta.

In February 2001, Jaswant Singh, then India's foreign minister, visited Burma to discuss avenues for closer cooperation. This was preceded by two visits to India by SPDC vice chairman Gen. Maung Aye in 2000 and followed by the first-ever visit to Burma by an Indian president. In March 2006, Abdul Kalam paid a four-day visit to Rangoon and highlighted the importance India placed on promoting closer connections with Burma.

While India had been cultivating ties with the pro-democracy movement, China had become an important ally of the Burmese government. This began already when on August 6, 1988, the two countries signed a bilateral border-trade agreement. By then the days of Mao Zedong's support to the CPB were well and truly over, and Deng Xiaoping's pragmatism was guiding Chinese foreign policy. The agreement was the first of its kind that hitherto isolated Burma had entered into with a neighbor. It was especially significant because it was signed at a time when Burma was in turmoil: two days later, the countrywide uprising broke out.

But the Chinese, renowned for their ability to plan far ahead, had expressed their intentions, almost unnoticed, in an article in the official weekly *Beijing Review* as early as September 2, 1985. Titled "Opening to the Southwest: An Expert Opinion." The article, which was written by the former vice minister of communications, Pan Qi, outlined the possibilities of finding an outlet for trade from China's landlocked provinces of Yunnan, Sichuan, and Guizhou, through Burma, to the Indian Ocean. It mentioned the Burmese railheads of Myitkyina and Lashio in the north and northeast, and the Irrawaddy River as possible conduits for the export of goods from those provinces, but omitted the fact that all relevant border areas at that time were not under Burmese central government control.

All that changed after the 1989 CPB mutiny, and the subsequent ceasefire agreements between the government and the Chinese-border-based insurgents. By late 1991, Chinese experts were assisting in a series of infrastructure projects to spruce up Burma's poorly maintained roads and railways. Border trade was booming, and China emerged as Burma's most important source of military hardware. Additional military equipment was provided by Pakistan, which also has helped Burma modernize its defense industries.

India, feeling that China's allies—Pakistan and Burma—were closing in on it in the west as well as the east, and wary of China's growing influence in Burma, dropped its support for the pro-democracy movement and began to woo the country away from its new backers in Beijing. Democracy and human rights were not part of the equation. Consequently, neither China nor India—Burma's two most powerful neighbors—would like to see another round of upheavals in Burma. Dealing with the "devil you know," the present government, is far easier than banking on a democratic administration that may or may not assume power sometime in the future.

In other words, Burma's future looks bleak. Its neighbors do not want to rock the status quo at the same time as the military is showing no signs of being interested in any kind of national reconciliation, or even talks with the pro-democracy movement. If there indeed is a reform-minded faction within the armed forces, as Min Zaw Oo suggests there is, it must be keeping an extremely low profile. On the other hand, Suu Kyi and the NLD have proven unable to bring the democratic movement any nearer its stated goals. Nor has it tried to reach out to any elements of the armed forces, or explain its policies to Burma's neighbors.

Time is running out for Burma. Economically, it is a total wreck, and it remains socially backwards. Since 1988, universities and colleges have been closed more than they have been open, and thousands of the country's brightest talents have left the country to look for a brighter future abroad. More than one hundred thousand people from the Karen, Mon, and Karenni minorities live in squalid refugee camps in Thailand. Drug abuse is rampant, especially in the border areas, and the HIV epidemic is out of control, probably more severe than in any other Southeast Asian country.

According to the World Health Organization (WHO), an estimated one in twenty-nine adults in Burma is living with HIV, and some 48,000 died from AIDS in the year 2000 alone. Malaria causes even more deaths, with over 700,000 cases reported in 2004. Dengue fever, tuberculosis, and other diseases are also widespread, and little is done about them. While the Burmese government is spending most of its budget on the military, only $22,000 was spent on a national aids control program in 2004. Burma allocates in total only 3 percent of its budget to health and 8 percent to education, while the military gets at least 50 percent.[40]

Until recently, the largest chunk of funding for disease control came from international donors. In August 2005, the Global Fund to Fight Aids, Tuberculosis and Malaria, the largest funder in Burma for HIV/AIDS control, withdrew because of onerous new restrictions laid down by the military government that made it impossible for foreign health workers to operate in the country.[41]

Arguing that Burma's health crisis and unsettled political situation pose a threat to regional security, the United States began to push for bringing the Burma issue before the UN Security Council—which could be a way forward—but met with stiff resistance against such a move from permanent members China and Russia. Japan, which is not a permanent member but sits on the Security Council, has also argued that the UN should not intervene in what is considered "an internal Burmese affair" with no relevance to regional security. More precisely, Japan—like India—does not want to antagonize the Burmese government, which they believe would drive it even further into the arms of the Chinese.

In September 2006, the Security Council finally agreed to "discuss" the Burma issue, but it is unlikely that any resolution will be passed, or action taken against the generals in Rangoon. The political stalemate is thus likely to continue for the foreseeable future. Burma is a country where everything seems to have gone wrong, and little can be done about it. The situation in Burma seems hopeless, with the military firmly entrenched in power and all opposition cowed into submission. The only hope that is a real hope lies with the emerging '88 Generation movement. In January 2007, Min Ko Kaing and those who had been arrested the previous September, were released, just as the '88 Generation launched yet another audacious campaign dubbed "Open Heart." It entailed a letter-writing campaign encouraging Burmese citizens across the country to write about their everyday complaints and grievances with military rule. When the month-long campaign ended in February, nearly twenty-five thousand letters had been sent to Than Shwe. That Min Ko Naing once again has ended up in prison does not mean that the dream of his generation—and older and younger people as well—is gone.

Given the strict restrictions on freedom of association and assembly, the '88 Generation may not morph into a full-blown political movement any time soon. But therein perhaps lies the nascent movement's strength: the military has shown that it is easy to squash a political party and detain its leaders, but it will be considerably more difficult to crush an entire generation.

Then there is the crucial role of the armed forces, which for better or for worse remains by far the country's most powerful institution. As potentially powerful a force as the '88 Generation may be, Min Zaw Oo is right: in the end, and as remote as the possibility may seem, real change is possible only when someone within the ruling military elite turns against the top leadership. This happened in the Philippines in 1986, when Ferdinand Marcos lost the support of his military; in Indonesia in 1998, when General Wiranto refused to storm the parliamentary buildings in Jakarta that had been occupied by pro-democracy activists; and in South Korea in 1979, when the democratic transition was set in motion by the assassination of President Park Chung-hee. Dictators do not negotiate their own demise, dictatorships never "reform" themselves through "dialogues" with their opponents, and they seldom fade away gradually.

Now it remains to be seen what Suu Kyi is going to do—and how the authorities are going to react if she embarks on another tour around the country, which most certainly will attract as many people as her rallies did in the 1990s. Her popularity has not waned, as anyone could see in the days after her 2010 release from house arrest. But she will not be able to push a pro-democracy agenda without the support of at least some elements within the armed forces. This is the bitter reality that she faces, as does the population at large and the international community.

BURMA: BASIC FACTS

Total area	676,578 square kilometers
Population	50,020,000 (2009 estimate)
Ethnic groups	Burman 68%; Shan 9%; Karen 7%; other ethnic minorities (Mon, Kachin, Chin, Karenni [Kayah], Arakanese [Rakhine], Naga, Wa, Chinese, Indians, and others) 16%
Religious groups	Buddhists 90%; Christians 5%; Muslims 4%
Capital	Naypyidaw (capital, or place of a king, in old-fashioned usage) near the central plains town of Pyinmana. The seat of government was moved from Rangoon in November 2005.
Government	Military dictatorship, although a bicameral parliament was elected on November 7, 2010
Administrative units	Seven divisions where the majority Burmans live (Rangoon, Irrawaddy, Magwe, Pegu, Tenasserim, Mandalay, Sagaing) and seven ethnic states (Karen, Karenni [Kayah], Shan, Kachin, Chin, Arakan [Rakhine], and Mon), but in terms of administration there is no difference between the divisions and the states. In 2010, the divisions were renamed regions.
Highest point	Hkakabo Razi, Kachin State, 5,881 meters
Main rivers	Irrawaddy, Chindwin, Salween
GDP per head	$571 (2009/2010 estimate; by comparison: China, $3,700; Thailand, $4,620; Bangladesh, $641; India, $1,124; Laos, $964)
Brief history	The ancient Burmese kingdom was conquered by the British in the three Anglo-Burmese wars of 1824–26, and 1885, and made a province of British India. It became a separate colony in 1937, fell under Japanese occupation in 1942–45, and became an independent republic in 1948. The military seized power in 1962, ending a fourteen-year experiment with federalism and parliamentary democracy.

AUNG SAN SUU KYI: A CHRONOLOGY

1945	June 19 - Born in Rangoon, daughter of national hero Aung San and Daw Khin Kyi
1950s	Attends the Methodist English High School in Rangoon
1960	Mother Khin Kyi appointed Burma's ambassador to India. Suu Kyi follows her to New Delhi, where she attends the Convent of Jesus and Mary and Lady Shri Ram College. Studies political science at Delhi University for two years.
1964–67	Studies philosophy, politics, and economics at St. Hugh's College, Oxford University. Earns a BA and works as a research assistant at the School of Oriental and African Studies.
1969–71	Works for the Advisory Committee on Administrative and Budgetary Questions at the UN secretariat in New York
1972	Marries Michael Aris. Works as a research officer at the Ministry of Foreign Affairs of the Kingdom of Bhutan
1973	First son, Alexander (Myint San Aung), is born after Suu Kyi and Michael have moved back to England.
1977	Second son, Kim (Htein Lin), is born
1985–86	Visiting scholar, Centre of Southeast Asian Studies, Kyoto
1987	Fellow, Indian Institute of Advanced Study, Simla, India
1988	April - Returns to Burma to look after her ailing mother
	July - Michael, Alexander, and Kim join her in Rangoon
	August 8 - A nationwide uprising for democracy sweeps across Burma. Thousands of unarmed demonstrators are gunned down by the military.
	August 26 - Makes her first public appearance. Half a million people come to listen to her outside the Shwe Dagon Pagoda in Rangoon.
	September 18 - The military steps in to reassert power. More unarmed demonstrators are gunned down by the army in Rangoon and elsewhere. The State Law and Order Restoration Council (SLORC) assumes power.

	September 27 - The National League for Democracy (NLD) is formed in Rangoon with Suu Kyi as its general secretary.
	December - Delivers hundreds of public addresses in Rangoon and up-country until July 1989.
1989	April 5 - Confronts an army unit at Danubyu, a small town in the Irrawaddy delta.
	July 20 - Placed under house arrest in Rangoon until July 10, 1995.
1990	May 27 - Despite her continuing detention, the NLD wins a landslide election victory, capturing 392 of 485 contested seats in the Pyithu Hluttaw (parliament), which, however, is never convened.
1991	July 10 - Awarded, in absentia, the 1990 Sakharov Prize (the European Parliament's human rights prize)
	October 14 - Awarded the 1991 Nobel Peace Prize. Her son Alexander receives it in Oslo on her behalf in December.
1995	July 10 - Released from house arrest. Begins weekly talks to large crowds outside the gate of her compound.
	November - NLD delegates, handpicked to sit with other, non-elected delegates in a "National Convention," withdraw from the body
1997	November 15 - SLORC becomes the State Peace and Development Council (SPDC)
1998	July–August - Tries to travel around the country, but is blocked by the military almost everywhere she goes
1999	March 27 - Michael Aris dies in London from prostate cancer
2000	September 23 - Second period of house arrest through May 6, 2002
2002	May 6 - Released from house arrest
	December 5 - The old dictator Ne Win dies in Rangoon.
2003	May 30 - Suu Kyi's entourage is attacked by a government-sponsored mob in Depayin in northern Burma. Scores of NLD supporters are killed.
	May 31 - Third period of house arrest through November 13, 2010

2006	May 18–20 - UN undersecretary-general for political affairs, Ibrahim Gambari, visits Rangoon, meets Suu Kyi, and leaves optimistic about Burma's future.
	May 27 - House arrest extended for another year
2007	September 22 - Buddhist monks and laypeople march past the barricades on the street leading to her house. She comes out of her house briefly to greet them. The next day, security is tightened around her house and no more visits allowed.
2009	May 14 - Charged with breaking the terms of her house arrest, which forbid visitors, after John Yettaw, an American, swims across to her house on the southern side of Inya Lake and refuses to leave. Yettaw is released but on August 11 Suu Kyi is sentenced to another eighteen months under house arrest.
2010	May 10 - NLD officially dissolved after refusing to register for the upcoming election, but continues to function as a political organisation.
	November 7 - Blatantly rigged elections are held for seats in Burma's new bicameral parliament as well as provincial and state assemblies. The military-supported Union Solidarity and Development Party (USDP) "wins" by a landslide.
	November 13 - Released from house arrest. Her son Kim visits her in Rangoon.

DRAMATIS PERSONAE

MICHAEL ARIS

Husband of Aung San Suu Kyi. Born in 1946 in Havana, Cuba, where his father worked for the British Council. Educated in England and an expert on Tibetan culture and the Himalayan region. Spent six years as the private tutor to members of the royal family of Bhutan. Married Aung San Suu Kyi in 1972. Was in Burma with Suu Kyi and their two sons, Alexander and Kim, during the 1988 uprising. Left the country a year later to lobby for his wife's cause. Diagnosed with prostate cancer in 1997 and died in Oxford on March 27, 1999.

AUNG GYI

Born in 1919 in Paungde, Prome district, of a Sino-Burmese family. Participated in the student movement in the 1930s and joined the anti-Japanese resistance in 1945. A close associate of Gen. Ne Win and member of the 1962 Revolutionary Council. Ousted in 1963 for his pragmatic policies. Influenced the 1988 movement by writing and widely distributing a series of letters to Ne Win. Briefly arrested in July–August. First chairman of the National League for Democracy on September 30. Broke away in December and set up his own Union Nationals Democracy Party in December. The party did not fare well in the 1990 election, winning only one seat. Now lives in retirement in Rangoon.

AUNG SAN

Father of Aung San Suu Kyi. Born in 1915 in Natmauk, Magwe. Key student leader in the 1930s. Left secretly for China and Japan in 1940 and returned to Burma on a mission to gather recruits for military training in Japan. The group, known as the "Thirty Comrades," set up the Burma Independence Army in Bangkok on December 26, 1941, and entered Burma with the Japanese soon afterwards. Later contacted the British and officially turned against the Japanese on March 27, 1945. Negotiated Burma's independence with the British on January 27, 1947.

Signed the Panglong Agreement with leaders of the Shan, Chin, and Kachin minorities on February 12. De facto prime minister of Burma until his assassination on July 19, 1947. Considered the father of Burma's independence and a national hero.

AUNG SAN U

Older brother of Aung San Suu Kyi. Born in 1943 in Rangoon. Left Burma for England in 1960. Now lives in San Diego, California. Has shown only scant interest in politics and has had quarrels with his sister about the ownership of the family home on University Avenue in Rangoon.

KHIN KYI

Mother of Aung San Suu Kyi. Born in 1912 in Myaungmya. A nurse by profession. Married Aung San in 1942. Leading member of the Women's Freedom League; Member of Parliament; chairman of the Social Planning Commission in 1953; chairman of the Council of Social Service; Burma's ambassador to India 1960–67. Died in Rangoon on December 27, 1988.

KHIN NYUNT

Born in 1939. Graduated from the Officers' Training School in Hmawbi in May 1960. Served as a military officer in Arakan and Karen States and was close to Ne Win. Appointed chief of the Directorate of the Defence Services Intelligence in 1983; secretary of the State Law and Order Restoration Council following the September 18, 1988, coup. Prime minister on August 23, 2003, until he was ousted and incarcerated on October 18, 2004. He was later transferred to house arrest.

KYI MAUNG

Born in 1918. Attended Rangoon University in 1937–40 and joined the student union under Aung San. Joined the nationalist forces in 1941 and studied at the Imperial Military Academy in Japan, 1943–45. Attended military training in Britain, 1947, and staff college at Fort Leavenworth, Kansas, US, 1955–56. Colonel and member of Ne Win's Revolutionary Council 1962; resigned in 1963. Retired from the army in 1964, joined the pro-democracy movement in 1988. Became NLD acting chairman following Suu Kyi's and Tin U's detention in July 1989. Led the NLD through the May 1990 election victory; detained in September for allegedly "passing state secrets to unauthorized persons." Had a conflict of opinion with Suu Kyi in 1997; died in August 2004.

MAUNG AYE

Born around 1940 at Kantbalu, Sagaing Division. Graduated from the Defence Services Academy in Maymyo in 1959. Northeastern commander in 1968; eastern commander in 1988. Member of the State Law and Order Restoration Council in 1988 and its deputy chairman in 1992. Has held the same position after the junta was renamed the State Peace and Development Council, in November 1997. Deputy Commander-in-Chief (Army).

DR. MAUNG MAUNG

Born in 1924 in Mandalay. Joined the Burmese nationalist forces during the Japanese occupation. Studied law in London and also attended the University of Utrecht in the Netherlands and Yale University in the US. Prolific writer and a prominent member of the Burma Socialist Programme Party. President of Burma, August 19–September 18, 1988. Later involved in drafting a new constitution. Died in Rangoon in 1994.

MIN KO NAING

At first a name which the students in Rangoon used for signing documents and statements during initial stages of the 1988 uprising; it means "Conqueror of kings" or "I shall defeat you." But since August 28 the nom de guerre for the most prominent student leader in Rangoon, Baw Oo Tun, then a twenty-six-year-old, third-year zoology student. Went underground in Rangoon after the September 18 coup. Arrested on March 24, 1989. Spent fifteen years in solitary confinement and was released in November 2004. Rearrested in September 2006, and later released. Arrested for the third time on August 21, 2007.

NE WIN

Born in 1911 in Paungdale, Prome district, of a Sino-Burmese family. Originally called Shu Maung. Attended Judson College in Rangoon but left without a degree in 1931. Post office clerk in Rangoon and a member of the Dohbama Asiayone in the 1930s. One of the "Thirty Comrades" and commander of the Burmese nationalist forces during most of the Japanese occupation. Commander-in-Chief, 1949–72. Prime minister in the Caretaker Government 1958–60. Seized power in a coup d'état on March 2, 1962; chairman of the Revolutionary Council, 1962–74; president of Burma, 1974–81; chairman of the Burma Socialist Programme Party from its inception to his resignation on July 23, 1988. Ruled from behind the scenes, but was gradually sidelined and placed under house arrest in March 2002. Died and was cremated without honors on December 5, 2002.

U NU

Born in 1907 in Wakema, Myaungmya district. Student leader in Rangoon in the 1930s. President of the Anti-Fascist Peoples Freedom League after Aung San's assassination on July 19, 1947. Prime minister, 1948–56, 1957–58, and 1960–62. In prison, 1962–66. Left Burma in 1969 and organized resistance against Ne Win's regime from Thailand, 1969–73. Then in exile in the US and India. Returned to Burma, 1980. Retired, but reemerged as a political leader during the 1988 uprising. Died in Rangoon in February 1995.

SANDA WIN

Born in 1952 in Rangoon. Daughter of Ne Win and his third wife, Khin May Than (Kitty Ba Than). Studied medicine in Rangoon, but failed her English-language exam when she wanted to further her studies in Britain in 1979—after which English education was reinstated in Burmese schools. Close to the country's military intelligence apparatus and believed to have played a major role in the crackdown on the movement of 1988. Later in business—hotels and entertainment—before she was placed under house arrest on March 7, 2002, along with her father, Ne

Win, her husband, Aye Zaw Win, and the couple's three sons. Now in private business in Rangoon.

SAW MAUNG

Born in 1928 in Mandalay. Joined the Burmese army in 1949. Vice Chief of Staff, 1983–84, Chief of Staff, 1985–92; first chairman of the State Law and Order Restoration Council, 1988–92. Became increasingly erratic, resigned for "health reasons" in April 1992, and died in obscurity in Rangoon on July 24, 1997.

SEIN LWIN

Born in a small village in the Moulmein area where he attended primary school. Joined the Burmese nationalist forces in 1943 and served under Ne Win. Killed Karen rebel leader Saw Ba U Gyi near the Thai border in 1950. Head of the security unit that massacred students at Rangoon University on July 7, 1962. Government minister and prominent member of the Burma Socialist Programme Party. President of Burma and chairman of the BSPP for eighteen days, from July 26 to August 12, 1988. Nicknamed "the Butcher" for his role in the August 1988 Rangoon massacre. Retired and died in poverty in Rangoon in April 2004.

SEIN WIN

Born in 1944 in Taungdwin Gyi. The son of U Ba Win, the elder brother of Aung San, he is Aung San Suu Kyi's cousin. Mathematician who graduated from Rangoon University and later obtained a doctorate in mathematics from Hamburg University. Taught in Sri Lanka and Kenya; returned to Burma in the mid-1980s. Joined the NLD in September 1988, then set up a sister party called the Party for National Democracy. Elected MP in the May 1990 election; fled to the Thai border in December where he and other MPs-elect founded the National Coalition Government of the Union of Burma (NCGUB). He was elected prime minister of the NCGUB; currently lives in the United States.

THAN SHWE

Born in 1933 in Kyaukse. Joined the army in 1953. Served in Shan State and in the southwest before becoming a member of the State Law and Order Restoration Council on September 18, 1988. Took over from Saw Maung in April 1992. Currently Burma's strongman with royal ambitions. In November 2005 he oversaw the move of the capital from Rangoon to Naypyidaw near Pyinmana.

TIN U

Born in 1927 in Bassein in the Irrawaddy delta. Chief of staff and minister of defense, 1974–76. Accused of involvement in an abortive coup attempt in July 1976 and imprisoned. Released in 1980 and took a degree in law. Emerged as one of the most popular pro-democracy leaders in 1988. One of the founders of the National League for Democracy. Under house arrest off and on, and arrested and sent to a prison in northwestern Burma in May 2003. Returned to house arrest in Rangoon in February 2004 and released from house arrest in February 2010.

ZARGANAR AKA THURA

Born in 1961 in Rangoon. A popular Burmese comedian, film actor, and film director. Originally a student of dentistry, he became famous for his biting, anti-government satires during the 1988 uprising (his stage name Zarganar can be translated as "forceps" or "tweezers"). He was arrested in 1988, then released, rearrested in 1990 during the election that year for ridiculing the government, and released again. On June 4, 2008, he was rearrested for speaking to foreign media about the situation of millions of people left homeless after Cyclone Nargis. He and other artists and entertainers had collected and sent relief supplies to the Irrawaddy delta, when the government was not doing anything. In November 2008, he was sentenced to fifty-nine years in prison. Currently in jail in the far north of the country.

NOTES

INTRODUCTION

1. A translation into English of her speech is in my possession.

2. Interview with a Burmese student who had fled to the Thai border after the crackdown in September 1988. Name withheld by mutual agreement.

3. BBC Summary of World Broadcasts (SWB), FE/0265 1, September 24, 1988.

4. "1990: Vote for Suu Kyi, against Ne Win," *Time International*, June 11, 1990, quoted in Philip Kreager, "Aung San Suu Kyi and the Peaceful Struggle for Human Rights in Burma," appendix in Aung San Suu Kyi, *Freedom from Fear and Other Writings* (London: Viking, 1991), 319.

5. SWB, Rangoon Home Service, July 27, 1990 (FE/0829 B/1, July 30, 1990).

6. *State Law and Order Restoration Council Chairman Commander-in-Chief of the Defence Services General Saw Maung's Addresses* (Rangoon, 1990), 323.

7. *Working People's Daily*, May 11, 1990.

8. Interview with U Hla Aung, Rangoon, April 1989. He also showed me charts and other documents he was working on.

9. A copy of the Gandhi Hall Declaration, dated July 29, 1990, is in my possession. The text is also available online from the Burma/Myanmar Online Library, http://www.burmalibrary.org/show.php?cat=1350&lo=t&sl=1, which directs to http://www.ibiblio.org/obl/docs/Gandhi_Hall_Declaration.htm.

10. A complete list of the wounded, beaten, and arrested monks is in my possession. The list was compiled by monks in Mandalay immediately after the incident.

11. SWB, August 8, 1990 (FE/0839 B/1, August 10, 1990).

12. "Report of the Committee on the Human Rights of Parliamentarians, 86th Inter-Parliamentary Conference, Santiago, Chile, October 7–12, 1991."

13. "Burmese Anti-govt Monks Told to Disband," *Bangkok Post*, October 21, 1990.

14. "Troops Storm 133 Mandalay Monasteries," *Bangkok Post*, October 23, 1990.

15. Mya Maung, *Totalitarianism in Burma: Prospects for Economic Development* (New York: Paragon House, 1992), 163.

16. Gustaaf Houtman, "Sacralizing or Demonizing Democracy: Aung San Suu Kyi's 'Personality Cult,'" in Monique Skidmore, ed., *Burma at the Turn of the 21st Century* (Honolulu: University of Hawaii Press, 2005), 145.

17. Aung San Suu Kyi, *The Voice of Hope: Conversations with Alan Clements* (London: Penguin Books, 1997), 75.

18. Aung San Suu Kyi, *Freedom from Fear and Other Writings* (London: Penguin Books, 1991), 231.

19. A videotape of the meeting is in my possession.

20. "We'll Play Fair: Interview with Kyi Maung," *Asiaweek*, July 13, 1990.

CHAPTER 1

1. For an outline of these beliefs, see Shway Yoe, *The Burman: His Life and Notions* (Arran, Scotland: Kiscadale Publications, 1989), 4–5.

2. Aung San, "Self-portrait," in Dr. Maung Maung, ed., *Aung San of Burma* (The Hague: Martinus Nijhoff [published for Yale University Southeast Asia Studies], 1962), 3.

3. Kin Oung, *Who Killed Aung San?* (Bangkok: White Lotus, 1993), 16–24.

4. Ibid., 20.

5. Aung San Suu Kyi, *Freedom from Fear and Other Writings* (London: Penguin Books, 1991), 144.

6. Ibid., 69.

7. Aung San Suu Kyi, *Burma and India: Some Aspects of Intellectual Life under Colonialism* (New Delhi: Allied Publishers, 1990), 71.

8. Ibid., 71.

9. Dr. Maung Maung, *Aung San*, 11.

10. Aung San Suu Kyi, *Burma and India*, 67.

11. Josef Silverstein, *Burma: Military Rule and the Politics of Stagnation* (Ithaca: Cornell University Press, 1977), 9–10.

12. Shway Yoe, *The Burman*, 286.

13. David I. Steinberg, "Literacy Tradition," *Far Eastern Economic Review*, November 27, 1987.

14. *A Brief History of the Dohbama Asiayone* [in Burmese] (Rangoon: Sarpay Beikman, 1976), 215. See also *The Guardian* monthly [in Burmese], Rangoon, February 1971: "The word *myanma* signifies only the Burmese whereas *bama* embraces all indigenous nationalities" (my translation).

15. *Working People's Daily*, May 27, 1989.

16. Aung San Suu Kyi, *Burma and India*.

17. Ibid., 71–72.

18. Kin Oung, *Who Killed Aung San*, 27.

19. Interview with Kyaw Zaw, Panghsang, January 1, 1987.

20. Won Z. Yoon, "Japan's Scheme for the Liberation of Burma: The Role of the Minami Kikan and the Thirty Comrades" (unpublished paper, Centre for International Studies, Ohio University, Athens, Ohio, 1973), 7–9.

21. Josef Silverstein, ed., *The Political Legacy of Aung San* (Ithaca: Cornell University Southeast Asia Program, 1993), 20–21.

22. Dr. Maung Maung, ed., *Aung San of Burma*, 47.

23. Kin Oung, *Who Killed Aung San*, 30.

24. F. S. V. Donnison, *British Military Administration in the Far East, 1943–45* (London: HMSO, 1956), 354.

25. Christopher Sykes, *Orde Wingate* (Cleveland: World Publishing Company, 1959), 403.

26. Quoted in Maurice Collis, *Last and First in Burma (1941–1948)* (London: Faber and Faber, 1956), 251.

27. *Tai Youth Magazine* (Rangoon University Shan Literary Society), No. 4, 1957.

28. Aung San Suu Kyi, *Freedom from Fear*, xvi.

29. Whitney Stewart, *Aung San Suu Kyi: Fearless Voice of Burma* (Minneapolis: Lerner Publications, 1997), 25.

30. Ibid., 20.

31. Ibid., 31. Michael Aris went through the family history when I visited him in Oxford in June 1989.

32. *Kuomintang Aggression Against Burma* (Rangoon: Khittaya Publishing House, 1951), 103–110. See also "The Secret War," in Bertil Lintner, *Burma in Revolt: Opium and Insurgency Since 1948,* 2nd ed. (Chiang Mai: Silkworm Books, 1999), 125–162.

33. Interview with Col. Michael Bremridge, British defense attaché in Rangoon, February 10, 1989.

34. See U Thaung, "Army's Accumulation of Economic Power in Burma (1950–1990)" (unpublished paper presented at Burma seminar, Washington D.C., October 20, 1990).

35. *The National Ideology and the Role of the Defence Services*, 3rd ed. (Rangoon, 1960).

36. I stayed with her husband Michael Aris in Oxford in June 1989 and had the privilege then of reading some of her personal writings.

37. Stewart, *Aung San Suu Kyi*, 37.

38. Ibid., 39.

39. See Inge Sargent, *Twilight over Burma: My Life as a Shan Princess* (Honolulu: University of Hawaii Press, 1994). Austrian-born Inge Sargent is Sao Kya Seng's widow.

40. See Robert Taylor, *The State in Burma* (London: C. Hurst, 1987).

41. For a more detailed account of what happened on the campus in July 1962, see Lintner, *Burma in Revolt*, 214–216.

42. Interview with Sein Win, Rangoon, April 1989.

43. Interviews and meetings with her old friends in Oxford, June 1989. Names withheld by mutual agreement.

44. Nalini Jain, "Her father's daughter," *Sunday Times* (Singapore), October 27, 1991.

45. Amnesty International, *Myanmar/Burma: Prisoners of Conscience: A Chronicle of Developments Since September 1988* (New York: Amnesty International, 1989), 59

46. Michael Aris, who passed away in March 1999, told me several times about their time in Bhutan, and showed me his photo albums.

47. Introduction by Michael Aris to Suu Kyi, *Freedom from Fear*, xvii.

48. Ibid.

49. For an excellent account of the unrest in Burma in the mid-1970s, see Andrew Selth, *Death of a Hero: The U Thant Disturbances in Burma, December 1974* (Brisbane: Griffith University, Centre for the Study of Australian-Asian Relations, 1989).

50. Alfred W. McCoy, *The Politics of Heroin in Southeast Asia* (New York: Harper and Row, 1972), 314.

51. Ibid., 336–337. See also *Focus* magazine (Bangkok), August 1981: "Only about 600 of the 1,374 men of the KKY in the Kokang region were paid by the government at a rate of 50 kyats [about US$7] per month. The remainder earned a living by trafficking in drugs or smuggling other goods."

52. Interview with Shan rebel leader Sao Hso Lane, Shan State, April 17, 1981.

53. Nalini Jain, "Her father's daughter."

54. Ibid.

55. Ibid.

56. Aung San Suu Kyi, *Aung San* (St. Lucia, Queensland: University of Queensland Press, 1984), later republished as *Aung San of Burma: A Biographical Portrait,* 2nd ed. (Edinburgh: Kiscadale Publications, 1991).

57. Aung San Suu Kyi, *Let's Visit Burma* (London: Burke Books, 1985).

58. Aung San Suu Kyi, *Burma and India.*

CHAPTER 2

1. From an unpublished account given to me by Peter Conard after the event. Also quoted in Bertil Lintner, *Outrage: Burma's Struggle for Democracy* (Hong Kong: Review Publishing, 1989), 131–32.

2. This account of what happened in August 1988 comes from my book *Outrage*, which was based on numerous interviews with pro-democracy activists who took part in the demonstrations and, after the September 18 crackdown, fled to Thailand. At the time, I compared those accounts with reports from several foreign embassies in Rangoon as well as with eyewitness accounts from observers such as Peter Conard.

3. "Burmese Take to Streets in Day of Protest," Associated Press report in *Bangkok Post*, August 9, 1988.

4. Interviews with Hmwe Hmwe and other activists, Bangkok, September–October 1988.

5. Seth Mydans, "Uprising in Burma: The Old Regime Under Siege", *New York Times*, August 12, 1988.

6. Interviews with Ko Lin (pseudonym) and his fellow students, Bangkok, October–November 1988.

7. Richard Gourley, "Troops Fire on Crowds in Rangoon," *Financial Times*, August 10, 1988.

8. Sit Naing (psuedonym) later fled to Thailand, returned to Burma, and was imprisoned in July 1989. He spent years in solitary confinement, then in a shared cell, before he was released in the late 1990s.

9. "Tourists Tell of Tears and Terror in Burma," *Bangkok Post*, August 11, 1988.

10. Interview with the visitors from Japan, September 1988. The following account of the Sagaing massacre is based on this interview and Gerry Abbott's *Back to Mandalay* (Bromley, Kent: Impact Books, 1990), 171–81, 216–18.

11. That teacher was Gerry Abbot. See also ibid., 171–81.

12. Summary of World Broadcasts FE/0227 B/1, Rangoon home service, 13:30 GMT, August 9, 1988.

13. US State Department, "Human Rights Statement," February 1989.

14. Lintner, *Outrage*, 104. This account is based on several interviews with medical volunteers, hospital personnel, and other eyewitnesses.

15. Dr. Maung Maung, *Burma and General Ne Win* (London: Asia Publishing House, 1969).

16. Quoted in Lintner, *Outrage*, 116; interview with Tin U, Rangoon, April 1989.

17. *Bangkok Post*, September 10, 1988.

18. "Ne Win Dumped by Independence Heroes," *Bangkok Post*, September 7, 1988.

19. These announcements were made public in independent newssheets, which circulated in Rangoon at the time. I have a large collection of these and other independent publications.

20. A copy of that issue of the *Phone Maw Journal*, informally published in August–September 1988, is in my possession.

21. "Note Verbale, Embassy of the Federal Republic of Germany, Rangoon/Burma, Wi 445 BIR 57/VN No. 318/88, October 28, 1988." The note continues, "The Embassy regrets to have to lodge a firm protest with the Government of Burma. It reserves all rights to later claim full compensation, on behalf of the Government of the Federal Republic of Germany, for the damage done to the Plant Protection and Rodent Control Project and for losses of public and damage incurred by the project." The Burmese foreign ministry replied on February 10, 1989, that it regretted "that the Embassy had to jump to the conclusion and lodged a formal protest." The German embassy reiterated their claim in an even more strongly worded Note Verbale dated March 8, 1989.

22. Copies of these leaflets are in my possession. English translations of the crude leaflets were compiled by the British Embassy in Rangoon at the time and circulated among the diplomatic community.

23. Capt. Si Thu was later promoted to major. In early 1993, he served as "guide and interpreter" for a visiting TV crew from Singapore.

24. Interview with Min Min, a twenty-two-year-old student from Burma, in Bangkok, October 15, 1988.

25. BBC Summary of World Broadcasts, Rangoon home service, 09:32 GMT, September 18, 1988.

26. Ibid., 11:23 GMT, September 18, 1988.

27. *The Nation* (Bangkok), May 25, 1990.

28. Melinda Liu, "Inside Burma: An On-Scene Report on the Crisis," *Newsweek*, October 3, 1988.

29. *Bangkok Post*, September 22, 1988.

30. *The Nation* (Bangkok), October 3, 1988.

31. A transcript of the talk is in my possession.

32. When I met Suu Kyi in Rangoon in April 1989, she had just returned from a tour of the Irrawaddy delta region. She told me that when she and her entourage had arrived at a small town that was accessible only by boat, the entire population came out to greet her and to take her to the local NLD office. There was a sign outside, a flag with the fighting peacock—the symbol of Burmese resistance—and, on the walls, portraits of her father and Thakin Kodaw Hmaing. "I was so surprised," she said. "We didn't know that there was an NLD office in that town."

33. *Programme of the National League for Democracy* (mimeograph), Rangoon, September 1988.

34. "Burmese Government Tells Parties to Obey Laws," *Bangkok Post*, December 20, 1988.

35. For a more detailed account of the foreign reaction to the massacres, see Lintner, *Outrage*, 144–45.

36. Kyaw Zwa Moe, "The Mother Who Was Overlooked," *Irrawaddy*, July 2006.

37. Ibid.

38. Whitney Stewart, *Aung San Suu Kyi: Fearless Voice of Burma* (Minneapolis: Lerner Publications, 1997), 88. See also, Lintner, *Outrage*, 172; *The Independent*, April 13, 1989; and *The New Yorker*, October 9, 1989.

39. "Burma Tightens Law on Printing, Publishing," *Bangkok Post*, June 20, 1989.

CHAPTER 3

1. "*Beyond Rangoon*," Wikipedia, last modified February 9, 2011, http://en.wikipedia.org/wiki/Beyond_Rangoon.

2. "Interview with [Adelle] Lutz," *Tricycle Magazine: Awake in the World* (online edition), Winter 1995, http://www.tricycle.com/special-section/adele-lutz.

3. Whitney Stewart, *Aung San Suu Kyi: Fearless Voice of Burma* (Minneapolis: Lerner Publications Company, 1997), 93.

4. Ibid., 94.

5. Barbara Bradley, "Dark Victory," *Vogue*, October 1995.

6. Stewart, *Aung San Suu Kyi*, 96.

7. Aung San Suu Kyi, *The Voice of Hope: Conversations with Alan Clements* (London: Penguin Books, 1997), 179–80.

8. Gustaaf Houtman, *Mental Culture in Burmese Crisis Politics: Aung San Suu Kyi and the National League for Democracy* (Tokyo: Tokyo University of Foreign Studies, Institute for the Study of Languages and Cultures of Asia and Africa, 1999), 279.

9. Quoted in ibid., 279.

10. Barbara Bradley, "Dark Victory."

11. Ibid.

12. Ibid.

13. Aung San Suu Kyi, *Freedom from Fear and Other Writings* (London: Penguin Books, 1991), 180. See also "Freedom from Fear," *Far Eastern Economic Review*, July 18, 1991.

14. Stewart, *Aung San Suu Kyi*, 108.

15. A transcript of what was discussed during the meeting is in my possession.

16. Josef Silverstein, "Burma's Woman of Destiny," in Aung San Suu Kyi, *Freedom from Fear*, 269.

17. Quoted in Mi Mi Khaing, *The World of Burmese Women* (London: Zed Books, 1984), 156.

18. Ma Thanegi is the author of *The Illusions of Life: Burmese Marionettes* (Bangkok: White Orchid Press, 1994).

19. Alexander Aris, "Speech of Acceptance Delivered on Behalf of Aung San Suu Kyi by Her Son Alexander Aris, on the Occasion of the Award of the Nobel Peace Prize in Oslo, December 10, 1991," at Nobelprize.org, The Official Web Site of the Nobel Prize, http://nobelprize.org/nobel_prizes/peace/laureates/1991/kyi-acceptance.html. I was also present at the occasion.

20. Ibid.

21. Bertil Lintner and Rodney Tasker, "General Malaise," *Far Eastern Economic Review*, February 13, 1992.

22. Ibid.

23. Ibid.

24. Bertil Lintner, "The Generals' New Clothes," *Far Eastern Economic Review*, November 25, 1993; see also, Bertil Lintner, "Repression Under Another Name," *Thailand Times*, January 15, 1994.

25. Lintner, "Repression Under Another Name."

26. Bertil Lintner, "Generals' Gambits," *Far Eastern Economic Review*, July 20, 1995.

27. Quoted in Bertil Lintner, "On Freedom's Way," *India Today*, August 15, 1995.

28. *Bangkok Post*, October 2, 1995.

29. "SLORC Says Suu Kyi Is a Traitor," *Irrawaddy*, December 16, 1995.

30. Ma Thanegi, "The Burmese Fairy Tale," *Far Eastern Economic Review*, February 19, 1998.

31. Ibid.

32. Dr. Kyi Maung Kaung, "Ms Ma Thanegi's Rules of Good Political Etiquette," *Irrawaddy Online Commentary*, November 23, 2001. http://www.irrawaddymedia.com/article.php?art_id=251.

33. The *Myanmar Times and Business Review* was set up in February 2000. The main Burmese partner was Col. Thein Swe, an air force officer and a member of the DDSI, as well as a close confidante of Khin Nyunt.

34. *Reuters*, Rangoon, December 12, 1997.

35. Ibid.

36. See Aung San Suu Kyi, *The Voice of Hope*. In August 2004, Kyi Maung suffered a heart attack and passed away. Regardless of his relationship with the NLD in his latter years, his death was a major setback to the opposition, as he had always been one of the most vital members of the country's pro-democracy movement. By the time of his death, hardly any of the original members of the party's executive board remained.

37. See "Obituary: A Courageous and Patient Man," *BBC News Online*, March 27, 1999.

38. Roger Mitton, "How Things Look Inside the NLD," *Asiaweek*, July 16, 1999.

39. Ibid.

40. Barbara Victor, *The Lady: Aung San Suu Kyi, Nobel Laureate and Burma's Prisoner* (New York: Faber and Faber, 1998), 222–23.

41. Aung San U, "The Bridges to Freedom in Burma" (Unpublished manuscript, 1990), 25.

42. Quoted in http://www.dassk.org, a website dedicated to Aung San Suu Kyi.

43. Aung Zaw, "Suu Kyi's Pilgrimage," *Irrawaddy Online*, June 18, 2002.

44. Gustaaf Houtman, "Sacralizing or Demonizing Democracy? Aung San Suu Kyi's 'Personality Cult,'" in *Burma at the Turn of the 21st Century*, ed. Monique Skidmore (Honolulu: University of Hawaii Press, 2005), 148.

45. Aung San Suu Kyi, *Letters from Burma* (London: Penguin Books, 1997), 13.

46. Ibid., 17.

47. Ibid., 160–61.

48. Houtman, *Mental Culture*, 282. The terms are in Pali, the canonical language of Buddhism, and concepts not usually associated with political struggles and strategies. Glossed, they are the four cardinal virtues or sublime states of mind, lovingkindness, compassion, perfection, mindfulness, insight, nirvana, arahant, and to awaken.

49. Ibid., 282.

50. Houtman, "Sacralizing or Demonizing Democracy," 149.

51. Aung San Suu Kyi, *The Voice of Hope*, 212–13.

52. Ibid., 9.

53. Aung San Suu Kyi, *Burma and India: Some Aspects of Intellectual Life under Colonialism* (New Delhi: Allied Publishers, 1990), 27.

54. For a detailed account of the incident, see Burma Lawyers' Council, "The Second Preliminary Report of the Ad Hoc Commission on Depayin Massacre (Burma)," (Thailand: Ad Hoc Commission on the Depayin Massacre, May 2004).

55. Ibid.

56. Ibid.

57. According to the website, "Daw Aung San Suu Kyi's Pages," "the military government has said that only 4 people were killed and 50 were injured in the incident but eyewitnesses and opposition groups in exile are stating that up to 70 people were killed and more than 200 people are missing and being detained." http://www.dassk.org/index.php?topic=628.0;wap2.

58. "Press Conference Clarifies Instigations to Cause Unrest Launched by Daw Suu Kyi of NLD and Followers Including U Tin Oo," *The New Light of Myanmar*, June 1, 2003, http://www.myanmar.gov.mm/NLM-2003/enlm/Jun01_h3.html.

CHAPTER 4

1. Bertil Lintner, "Myanmar Payback Time," *Jane's Defence Weekly*, April 20, 2005.

2. See Benedict Rogers, *Than Shwe: Unmasking Burma's Tyrant* (Chiang Mai: Silkworm Books, 2010).

3. *Irrawaddy*, April 2006. I have changed the spelling of the names of the kings to accord with the standard form of Romanization.

4. Aung Zaw, "Retreat to the Jungle," *Irrawaddy*, December 2005. The move took place in November.

5. Edward Loxton, "Off-Limits—Asia's Secret Capital," *Citylife* (Chiang Mai), June, 2006.

6. Clive Parker, "A Tale of Two Cities," *Irrawaddy Online*, August 24, 2006.

7. Bertil Lintner, "Myanmar and North Korea Share a Tunnel Vision," *Asia Times Online*, July 19, 2006.

8. Ibid.

9. Aung Zaw, "Retreat to the Jungle."

10. Burmese Broadcasting Service, monitored by BBC, FE/0265i, September 24, 1988.

11. Interview with Harn Yawnghwe, son of Burma's first president, Sao Shwe Thaike (who was a Shan), in Bertil Lintner, "Cultural Revolution," *Far Eastern Economic Review*, November 18, 1999.

12. Gustaaf Houtman, *Mental Culture in Burmese Crisis Politics: Aung San Suu Kyi and the National League for Democracy* (Tokyo: Tokyo University of Foreign Studies: Institute for the Study of Languages and Cultures of Asia and Africa), 1999, 55ff.

13. Quoted in ibid., 143.

14. Burma's generals are often described as inept and misguided leaders propelled by superstition rather than rational thinking. When the capital was shifted to Naypyidaw, 320 kilometers north of Rangoon, the official move apparently took place at 6:36 a.m. on November 6, 2005, a time that had been selected by stargazers. Five days later, at 11 a.m. on November 11, a second convoy of 1,100 military trucks carrying eleven military battalions and eleven government ministries left Rangoon for the new capital. The significance of those numbers is not entirely clear, but many ordinary people in Burma will tell you that the generals are not only kings isolated from their subjects, but also deeply delusional. To guarantee their continuing rule they are said to believe that the intervention of spirits is necessary—in case their strong-arm tactics fail—and to rely on astrologers, mediums, and soothsayers to help make important decisions about the country's future.

Characteristically, two decades earlier, on September 22, 1987, all old banknotes were rendered worthless and replaced by 45 and 90 kyat bills. The new currency proved a nightmare for consumers and vendors as well as Burma's few foreign investors, who, after 1988, began to discover the country's vast resources of gems and minerals. The government then issued 20, 50, 100 and 500 kyat banknotes, along with a 50 pya note (100 pyas equals one kyat), the equivalent of less than a twentieth of a US cent. There was a reason for its introduction: 20+50+100+500+50=720 and 7+2+0=9, a number considered lucky in Burma. The 50 pya denomination may have all but disappeared but now there exists a 5,000 kyat banknote (50+0+0=50), which does the same trick.

All important decisions are also made on auspicious dates, which add up to or are divisible by nine. The State Law and Order Restoration Council assumed power on October 18, 1988 (1+8=9); the name of the country was changed to Myanmar from Burma on May 27, 1989 (2+7=9); Aung San Suu Kyi was first placed under house arrest on July 20, 1989 (7+2+0=9); the general election was held on May 27, 1990 (2+7=9); Khin Nyunt was ousted and incarcerated on October 18, 2004 (1+8=9); and the move to Naypyidaw was first officially announced on November 7, 2005 (11+7=18 and 1+8=9).

15. Josef Silverstein, *Burmese Politics: The Dilemma of National Unity* (Brunswick, NJ: Rutgers University Press, 1980), 14.

16. Robert Taylor, *The State of Burma* (London: C. Hurst, 1987), 100.

17. Houtman, *Mental Culture*, 100.

18. Aung San Suu Kyi, *Freedom from Fear*, 231.

19. *The White Shirts: How USDA Will Become the New Face of Burma's Dictatorship*, (Mae Sot: Network for Democracy and Development, May 2006), 18.

20. Houtman, *Mental Culture*, 117.

21. *White Shirts*, 18–19.

22. Houtman, *Mental Culture*, 118.

23. Burmese radio recorded by FBIS, May 16, 1996.

24. *White Shirts*, 53.

25. Ibid., 55.

26. Ibid., 56.

27. Houtman, *Mental Culture*, 118.

28. Leslie Kean and Dennis Bernstein, "Aung San Suu Kyi: The Progressive Interview," *BurmaNet News*, March 1997, quoted in Houtman, *Mental Culture*, 199.

29. Ibid.

30. *White Shirts*, 35.

31. Ibid., p. 26; David Steinberg, "The Union Solidarity and Development Organization," *Burma Debate*, January/February 1997.

32. *White Shirts*, 69–72.

33. *Burma Debate*, January/February 1997.

34. Larry Jagan, "Another Unhappy Birthday in Myanmar," *Asia Times Online*, June 20, 2006.

35. Debbie Kreuser, "Walk On: Bono and the Lady," *HelloAngel*, May 28, 2004.

36. Press release, "For the Lady," Carla Sacks & Co., September 20, 2004.

37. This and following quotes from Aung Zaw, "Than Shwe: Burma's Strrongman?" *Irrawaddy*, January–February 2003.

38. "Rolling the Bones," *Irrawaddy*, September 2006.

39. "Tracking the Tycoons," *Irrawaddy*, September 2005.

40. Ibid.

41. Clive Parker, "An Assured Political Future," *Irrawaddy*, March 2006.

42. Ibid.

43. See numerous articles in *The New Light of Myanmar* that use this phrase.

44. Aung San Suu Kyi, *Letters from Burma* (London: Penguin Books, 1997), 152.

45. *Eight Seconds of Silence: The Death of Democracy Activists Behind Bars* (Mae Sot: Assistance Association for Political Prisoners, May 2006), 52–53.

46. Moe Aye, *Ten Years On: The Life and Views of a Burmese Student Political Prisoner* (Bangkok, March 1999), 101.

47. Ibid., 108.

48. Ibid., 101.

49. "Medical Concern: Death in Custody of Leo Nichols," *Amnesty International*, July 16, 1996.

50. This and other cases of death in custody are taken from *Eight Seconds of Silence*.

51. Aung San Suu Kyi, *Letters from Burma*, 147.

52. Ibid., 151.

53. *Eight Seconds of Silence*, 24.

54. *The Darkness We See: Torture in Burma's Interrogation Centres and Prisons* (Mae Sot: Assistance Association for Political Prisoners, December 2005), 63.

55. Ibid., 32.

56. *Eight Second of Silence*, 25.

57. *Burma Debate*, March 2003.

58. Marwaan Macan-Markar, "Myanmar Boots Out Western Peacemakers," *Asia Times Online*, March 10, 2006.

59. "UN Says Burmese Dissident May Go Free Soon," *Voice of America*, May 24, 2006.

60. See note 14 in this chapter.

CHAPTER 5

1. A copy of the Gandhi Hall Declaration, dated July 29, 1990, is in my possession. The text is also available online from the Burma/Myanmar Online Library, http://www.burmalibrary.org/show.php?cat=1350&lo=t&sl=1, which directs to http://www.ibiblio.org/obl/docs/Gandhi_Hall_Declaration.htm.

2. Confidential interview with an Indian diplomat, Bangkok, December 10, 1990.

3. Jason Vest, "From Green Bay to U.S. Flacks Spread Goodwill for Burma's Junta," *The Progressive*, November 1996.

4. Ibid.

5. These are American estimates. See Bertil Lintner, *Burma in Revolt: Opium and Insurgency Since 1948* (Chiang Mai: Silkworm Books, 2003), v; *International Narcotics Control Strategy Report* (Washington, DC: US Department of State, 1987, 1998, and 1995).

6. "US Department of Justice: Registration Statement 3690," February 9, 1993.

7. John Barron, *KGB Today: The Hidden Hand* (London: Hodder and Stoughton, 1983), 254.

8. "Report to the Honest Ballot Association Regarding Narcotics and Human Rights in Myanmar, May 6, 1993." (New York: Honest Ballot Association, 1993). The report was signed by Donald A. MacDonald, Seymour Halpern, and Robert Leggett. Halpern and Leggett are former US congressmen.

9. A copy of the report is in my possession.

10. Bertil Lintner, "Velvet Glove," *Far Eastern Economic Review*, May 7, 1998.

11. See, for instance, Tony Emerson, "Inside Burma's Golden Triangle: Despite the War on Poppies, There's Plenty of Drug Money Around," *Newsweek* (Asian edition), April 20, 1998.

12. Sen. Mitch McConnell, letter to the editor, *Washington Post*, February 28, 2003.

13. A transcript of Burton Levin's speech is in my possession.

14. I have met numerous UN officials and Western diplomats and businessmen who have voiced such arguments.

15. M. S. Dobbs-Higginson, *Asia Pacific: Its Role in the New World Disorder* (Kew, Australia: Mandarin Books, 1996), 377.

16. Ibid., 379–80.

17. Ibid., 394.

18. Aung San Suu Kyi glosses over the incident in her book about her father, *Aung San of Burma* (Edinburgh: Kiscadale Publications, 1991), 39–40.

19. "More than One Million Ethnic Civilians Forcibly Displaced by Burma's Military Dictatorship," Church World Service, September 28, 2006.

20. Jim Andrews, "We Are the Front Line," *Irrawaddy*, December 2005.

21. Ibid.

22. Quoted in "The Spirit of '88 Lives," *Irrawaddy*, September 2006.

23. I came across these statements while working on a report on the Burmese media for the Southeast Asia Press Alliance in 2006.

24. Marwaan Macan-Markar, "Hints of a 'Velvet Revolution,'" Inter Press Service News Agency, October 30, 2006.

25. Jim Andrews, "We Are the Frontline: The 1988 Generation a Force to Reckon With," *Irrawaddy*, December 2005.

26. See Kenneth Denby, "The World Is Watching Burma Over Aid Pledges," *The Times/Sunday Times*, May 26, 2008, http://www.timesonline.co.uk/tol/news/world/asia/article4004176.ece; see also, "World Tells Myanmar to Focus on Saving Lives," Agence France Presse, May 26, 2008.

27. Human Rights Watch, "Vote to Nowhere," April 30, 2008, http://www.hrw.org/en/node/62239/section/5.

28. "Interview: Tin Oo Says Election Most Unpopular Ever," *Irrawaddy*, November 6, 2010, http://www.irrawaddy.org/article.php?art_id=19974.

29. For reports on the rigged 2010 election, see *Irrawaddy*, November 10, 2010, http://www.irrawaddy.org/election/news/603-NUP-concedes-defeat.html, and *Christian Science Monitor*, November 7, 2010, http://www.csmonitor.com/World/Asia-South-Central/2010/1107/Burma-Myanmar-holds-first-vote-in-20-years.

30. *Constitution of the Republic of the Union of Myanmar* (Rangoon: Printing and Publishing Enterprise, Ministry of Information, 2008).

31. Yeni, "Local Media Barred from Publishing Suu Kyi Interviews," *Irrawaddy*, December 17, 2010, http://*www.irrawaddy.org/article.php?art_id=20340.*

32. See Myanmar Egress website, http://www.myanmaregress.org/.

33. Zin Linn, "The Advocates of Burma's Unfair Election," *Asian Correspondent.com*, September 21, 2010, http://asiancorrespondent.com/40545/the-advocates-of-burma%E2%80%99s-unfair-polls-in-november/.

34. David Mathieson, "Burma's Elections: Towards Realistic Hope," OpenDemocracy website, November 24, 2010, http://www.opendemocracy.net/david-scott-mathieson/burma%E2%80%99s-elections-towards-realistic-hope.

35. This concept has been promoted by many of her foreign supporters. See, for instance, the coffee-table book by Alan Clements and Leslie Kean, *Burma's Revolution of the Spirit: The Struggle for Democracy, Freedom and Dignity* (New York: Aperture Foundation, 1994).

36. Quoted in Gustaaf Houtman, *Mental Culture in Burmese Crisis Politics: Aung San Suu Kyi and the National League for Democracy* (Tokyo: Tokyo University of Foreign Studies, Institute for the Study of Languages and Cultures of Asia and Africa, 1999), 301.

37. Ibid., 302.

38. Min Zaw Oo, "When the Sky Collapses: Strategic Simulation of State Failure in Burma and Its Consequences," April 20, 2006, http://groups.yahoo.com/group/burmanewsgroup/message/2033.

39. Associated Press and the BBC, May 7, 2005.

40. "Threat to Peace: A Call for the UN Security Council to Act in Burma," Report Commissioned by Vaclav Havel and Bishop Desmond M. Tutu, prepared by law firm, DLA, Piper Rudnick, Gray Cary, September 20, 2005, http://www.dlapiper.com/us/publications/detail.aspx?pub=5647.

41. Min Zaw Oo, "When the Sky Collapses."

SUGGESTED READING

Aung San Suu Kyi. *Aung San of Burma: A Biographical Portrait*. 2nd ed. Edinburgh: Kiscadale, 1991.
A biography of Aung San written by his daughter.

———. *Burma and India: Some Aspects of Intellectual Life Under Colonialism*. New Delhi: Allied Publishers, 1990.
A useful account of the early years of Burmese nationalism.

———. *Freedom from Fear and Other Writings*. London: Penguin Books, 1991.
An anthology of writings by Aung San Suu Kyi.

———. *Letters from Burma*. London: Penguin Books, 1997.
A collection of letters which were previously published as a weekly series in the Japanese daily *Mainichi Shimbun*.

———. *The Voice of Hope: Conversations with Alan Clements*. London: Penguin Books, 1997.
A question-answer session with former Buddhist monk Alan Clements.

Aye Kyaw. *The Voice of Young Burma*. Ithaca: Cornell University, Southeast Asia Program, 1993.
A history of the Burmese student movement in the 1920s and 1930s.

Becka, Jan. *Historical Dictionary of Burma*. Metuchen, NJ: Scarecrow Press, 1995.
Covers events, personalities and organizations in dictionary format.

———. *The National Liberation Movement in Burma During the Japanese Occupation Period (1941–1945)*. Prague: The Oriental Institute in Academia, 1983.
A well-researched account of the development of Burmese nationalism under Japanese occupation.

Callahan, Mary. *Making Enemies: War and State Building in Burma*. Ithaca: Cornell University Press, 2003.
An academic study of the Burmese military and its role in politics.

Charney, Michael W. *A History of Modern Burma*. Cambridge: Cambridge University Press, 2009.
A well-researched account of Burma's modern history by a senior lecturer in the Department of History, School of Oriental and African Studies, London.

Fink, Christina. *Living Silence: Burma Under Military Rule*. London: Zed Books, 2001.
A portrait of Burmese society under military rule, and an account of how the military has managed to maintain itself in power.

Houtman, Gustaaf. *Mental Culture in Burmese Crisis Politics: Aung San Suu Kyi and the National League for Democracy*. Tokyo: Tokyo University of Foreign Studies, Institute for the Study of Languages and Cultures of Asia and Africa, 1999.
Deals with the Buddhist dimensions underlying the politics of Aung San Suu Kyi and the Burmese democracy movement in general.

Izumiya Tatsuro. *The Minami Organ*. Translated by U Tun Aung Chain. Rangoon: Arts and Science University Press, 1981.
An account of the Japanese occupation as seen from a Japanese perspective.

Khin Yi. *The Dobama Movement in Burma (1930–1938)*. Ithaca: Cornell University Southeast Asia Program, 1988.
About the early years of the Burmese nationalist movement.

Kin Oung. *Who Killed Aung San?* Bangkok: White Lotus, 1996.
Provides a graphic reconstruction of events leading up to the assassination of Aung San in 1947 as well as its aftermath.

Larkin, Emma. *Secret Histories: Finding George Orwell in a Burmese Teashop*. London: John Murray, 2004.
A journey into the Orwellian land that Burma's ruling generals have created.

Lintner, Bertil. *Burma in Revolt: Opium and Insurgency since 1948*. Chiang Mai: Silkworm Books, 2003.
A history of Burma's civil strife and the interrelated trade in illicit narcotics.

———. *Outrage: Burma's Struggle for Democracy*. London: White Lotus, 1990.
An account of the 1988 pro-democracy uprising in Burma. It also contains notes on the civil war and the ethnic minorities.

Lintner, Bertil, and Michael Black. *Merchants of Madness: The Methamphetamine Explosion in the Golden Triangle*. Chiang Mai: Silkworm Books, 2009.
About the dramatic increase in the methamphetamine production in Burma over the past two decades.

Marshall, Andrew. *The Trouser People*. London: Viking, 2002.
A powerful exposé of the tragedy of modern Burma.

Maung Maung, Dr., ed. *Aung San of Burma*. The Hague: Martinus Nijhoff (for Yale University Southeast Asia Studies), 1962.
A collection of essays about Aung San by various Burmese and some British writers.

———. *Burma and General Ne Win*. Bombay: Asia Publishing House, 1969.
A sycophantic biography of Ne Win by the Burmese military's official historian.

———. *The 1988 Uprising in Burma*. New Haven: Yale University, Center for Southeast Asia Studies, 1999.

An unconvincing attempt to explain that what happened in 1988 was not a popular uprising but some kind of "disturbance."

Maung Maung, (ex-Brig.-Gen.). *Burmese Nationalist Movements 1940–1948.* Edinburgh: Kiscadale, 1990.
A well-researched account of Burma's struggle for independence, and the various parties and personalities in the 1940s.

Maung Maung Gyi. *Burmese Political Values: The Socio-Political Roots of Authoritarianism.* New York: Praeger Publishers, 1983.
An excellent account of the historical origins of authoritarian rule in Burma.

Mya Maung. *The Burma Road to Poverty.* New York: Praeger Publishers, 1991.
A detailed description and analysis of military misrule in Burma by a Boston-based Burmese economist.

———. *Totalitarianism in Burma: Prospects for Economic Development.* New York: Paragon House, 1992.
A similar study of the disastrous policies of Burma's military rulers.

Rogers, Benedict. *Than Shwe: Unmasking Burma's Tyrant.* Chiang Mai: Silkworm Books, 2010.
So far the only biography of Burma's strongman, Gen. Than Shwe.

Sarkisyanz, E. *Buddhist Background of the Burmese Revolution.* The Hague: Martinus Nijhoff, 1965.
A study of Burmese political thought and intellectual history.

Shway Yoe. *The Burman: His Life and Notions.* Arran, Scotland: Kiscadale Publications, 1989 (reprint).
A timeless classic about Burmese culture actually written by Sir J. G. Scott, an Englishman.

Selth, Andrew. *Burma's Armed Forces: Power Without Glory.* Norwalk, CT: East-Bridge, 2002.
A scholarly account of the Burmese military and the country's defense policies.

Silverstein, Josef. *Burma: Military Rule and the Politics of Stagnation.* Ithaca: Cornell University Press, 1977.
A comprehensive introduction to modern Burmese politics.

———. *Burmese Politics: The Dilemma of National Unity.* New Brunswick, NJ: Rutgers University Press, 1980.
An analysis of Burma's struggle for national unity up to the military takeover in 1962.

———, ed. *Independent Burma at Forty Years: Six Assessments.* Ithaca: Cornell University Southeast Asia Program, 1989.
An assessment of Burma's political development since independence in 1948 by six different scholars.

———, ed. *The Political Legacy of Aung San*. Ithaca: Cornell University Southeast Asia Program, 1993.
A collection of documents about and by Aung San.

Smith, Martin. *Burma: Insurgency and the Politics of Ethnicity*. London: Zed Press, 1991.
A detailed study of Burma's ethnic strife, which, unfortunately, contains many inaccuracies and factual errors.

Steinberg, David. *Burma: A Socialist Nation of Southeast Asia*. Boulder, CO: Westview Press, 1982.
A useful introduction to various aspects of Burmese history and politics.

———. *Burma: The State of Myanmar*. Washington, DC: Georgetown University Press, 2001.
About political developments in Burma after the 1988 pro-democracy uprising.

———. *Burma's Road Toward Development: Growth and Ideology Under Military Rule*. Boulder, CO: Westview Press, 1981.
Paints a fairly rosy picture of economic growth in Burma in the 1970s.

———. *The Future of Burma: Crisis and Choice in Myanmar*. Lanham, NY: University Press of America, 1990.
An account of Burma's political crisis in the late 1980s and the emergence of the National League for Democracy.

Stewart, Whitney. *Aung San Suu Kyi: Fearless Voice of Burma*. Minneapolis: Lerner Publications, 1997.
A respectful biography of Aung San Suu Kyi written for secondary-school students.

Taylor, Robert H. *The State in Burma*. London: C. Hurst, 1987.
An account of political developments in Burma written from a pro-regime point of view.

Thant Myint-U. *The Making of Modern Burma*. Cambridge: Cambridge University Press, 2001.
A scholarly account of developments that led to independence for Burma.

———. *The River of Lost Footsteps: Histories of Burma*. New York: Farrar, Straus and Giroux, 2006.
A personal history of Burma and the author's family.

Tinker, Hugh. *Burma: The Struggle for Independence 1944–1948*. London: Her Majesty's Stationery Office, 1984.
An almost complete collection of documents on Burma's relations with Britain during the years immediately before independence.

———. *The Union of Burma*. London: Oxford University Press, 1957.
A comprehensive history of Burma in the late 1940s and the 1950s.

Trager, Frank. *Burma: From Kingdom to Republic*. London: Pall Mall Press, 1966.
A historical and political analysis of modern Burma.

———, ed. *Japanese Military Administration, Selected Documents, 1941–1945*. Philadelphia: University of Pennsylvania Press, 1971.
Edited translations of documents from the Japanese occupation period.

Tucker, Shelby. *Burma: The Curse of Independence*. London: Pluto Press, 2001.
An account of Burma's cultural diversity, and how the Burmese military has turned a once prosperous state into an economic and political wreck.

Victor, Barbara. *The Lady: Aung San Suu Kyi, Nobel Laureate and Burma's Prisoner*. New York: Faber and Faber, 2002.
A rather heroic account of Aung San Suu Kyi's role in the struggle for democracy in Burma.

Wintle, Justin. *Perfect Hostage: A Life of Aung San Suu Kyi*. London: Hutchinson, 2007.
A detailed biography of Aung San Suu Kyi.

Won Z. Yoon. *Japan's Scheme for the Liberation of Burma: The Role of the Minami Kikan and the "Thirty Comrades."* Ohio University: Center for International Studies, 1973.
A valuable academic study of Japan's involvement with the Burmese nationalist movement.

[illegible] and political [illegible]

[illegible] University of [illegible] Press.

[illegible]

[illegible] and how the [illegible]

[illegible]

[illegible]

[illegible]

[illegible]

INDEX